**Stories and Songs of Faith:
My Journey with God**

A 52-Week Devotional
by
Alexis A. Goring

Copyright © 2021 Alexis A. Goring
Published by Writer at Heart Editorial Services
Unless otherwise noted, scriptures are taken from the King James Version

Other Bible translations used:

THE HOLY BIBLE, NEW INTERNATIONAL VERSION®, NIV® Copyright © 1973, 1978, 1984, 2011 by Biblica, Inc.® Used by permission. All rights reserved worldwide.

Scripture quotations marked as NRSV are from the New Revised Standard Version Bible, copyright © 1989 the Division of Christian Education of the National Council of the Churches of Christ in the United States of America. Used by permission. All rights reserved.

Scripture quotations marked TPT are from The Passion Translation®. Copyright © 2017, 2018 by Passion & Fire Ministries, Inc. Used by permission. All rights reserved. ThePassionTranslation.com.

Scripture quotations marked NLT are taken from the *Holy Bible*, New Living Translation, copyright © 1996, 2004, 2015 by Tyndale House Foundation. Used by permission of Tyndale House Publishers, Inc., Carol Stream, Illinois 60188.

All rights reserved.
ISBN: 978-1-7369795-2-5

April 2024

Dedication

I dedicate this devotional book to you (the reader). I am praying that God will use this message to be a blessing for your heart.

Dear Christina James,
thank you for your Bright FM radio station ministry. You are a blessing to all of your listeners. I hope my devotional book here will be a blessing to you ♡ May God bless you and keep you close to Him.
Love, Alexis A. Porero

Endorsements

"Alexis's passion to compose heartfelt and inspired writings through this devotional is refreshment to the soul. May your day-to-day be edified by her writings and warm blessings." – *Jenn Gotzon*, award-winning actress, producer and speaker

"For years, I've started almost every day with a spiritual devotion and it is as important as breakfast. I'm ready to face the day when I've had a word from God. In this book, Alexis brings a balanced table of stories from life, scripture, and challenges to combat the prophecy in Amos 8:11 that there would be a famine of hearing the words of the Lord. Read. Eat!" – *Ada Brownell*, Christian author

"With God as our Guide, Alexis takes us to places of faith, renewal, belonging, hope, light, love, and life. Each stop along her personal journey with God inspires us to remember our own stories of faith within God's bigger story. These are places you will want to visit or revisit. Songs you will want to sing. And a 52-week trip you don't want to miss." – *Karen "Girl" Friday*, writer, speaker, pastor's wife, blogger

"Alexis A. Goring takes us on a journey of faith in action that will surely resonate with readers." – *Chandra Sparks Splond*, author and blogger

"God has profoundly touched my life through Alexis A. Goring's uplifting and personable weekly devotional book sharing God's love through her own experiences and insights. It is so well written and in a voice that feels as if a close friend is having coffee with you and talking of God. Every entry is backed by Scripture, as well as highlights meaningful songs that God has used to touch the author's heart. As a fellow journalist, I love how the author uses her talent of observation to see God at work all around her as well as the use of thought-provoking questions at each devotional's end to further connect our lives to that entry's theme and the Scripture truth it has been based on. If you are looking for a devotional that is short but powerful, this is it. It would be a perfect gift for a special person in your life." – *Morgan Tarpley Smith*, award-winning journalist and aspiring author

"Filled with heartfelt, personal reflection, Alexis A. Goring explores our journey through life in faith. Sprinkled with songs for joy and pain, this devotional can be a welcome respite for your soul." – *Allison M. Wilson*, author and editor

"Alexis A. Goring has a way of drawing you into the story and guiding you through how much you are valued by the Creator. It's like she's taking you by the hand, leading you through a beautiful garden, pointing out God's glory and His love for you. If you're ever doubting how much you're loved by God, each devotion reminds you how He's got you covered." – *Becky Alignay*, host of *Middays with Becky* on WGTS 91.9 FM

"This devotional book is a perfect weekly guide to a closer walk with our Savior and an in-depth view of His desire to shower us with His love." – *Naeem Newman, M.D.*

"Both wise and uplifting, *Stories and Songs of Faith* is grounded in real life experience. The devotionals ring true and so does the depth of Alexis's faith. Her words are like tempered steel—strong, tested, and enduring. Highly recommended!" – *Victoria Bylin*, award-winning author

"Alexis A. Goring has written a devotional filled with true life experiences. *Stories and Songs of Faith: My Journey with God* will make you rethink the path you are walking and long to deepen your relationship with Jesus!" – *Terri Weldon*, award-winning author of *The Christmas Bride Wore Boots*

"Through this devotional, Alexis provided great practical analogies from her life to cover deep subjects. She gave us all a glimpse of the Father's heartbeat for humanity—relationship and intimacy. A delightful read for any season of life." – *Valeria Hyer*, aspiring author, wife, mother, book reader

"Practical, concise and soulful. Alexis A. Goring has compiled a series of devotional readings that I found to be thought-provoking and spiritually challenging, in a good way. The questions at the end of each devotional pushed me beyond merely reading the text. I had to give thought to what was written, not only on the paper pages but on the leaves of my

heart, my soul and my mind. Theologically balanced, each devotional was fruitful prose in due season."
– *Chaplain Paul S. Anderson, D.Min.*, Director of Adventist Chaplaincy Ministries

"With thoughtful care and conversational tone, Alexis plucks encouragement from her everyday life in this collection of devotions. She offers practical tools and welcomes the reader to explore and reflect on the spiritual concepts she discusses in their own lives. Alexis invites the reader to take a journey—one that she has herself taken—and each week she leaves another precious breadcrumb on the trail. Faith and hope are present on every page." – *Quantrilla Ard*, writer and encourager, The PhD Mamma

"I love each of the scriptures. The refreshing, real-life stories and reflections she shares are perfect illustrations that prove how relevant the Bible is in today's world—its wisdom is timeless, as is every story. Each week closes with questions that hold me accountable in my faith walk. I highly recommend this devotional." – *Cathy Oasheim*, Christian editor

"Through real life experiences and practical applications of the Bible, Alexis takes you on a colorful spiritual journey that is inspiring, musical, educational, and awesome! With discussion questions at the end of each week, she challenges the reader to reflect, dig deep, and enjoy your walk with Jesus."
– *Heather "Chef Mommy" Martin*, Virtue music group singer

"Alexis A. Goring's devotional book, *Stories and Songs of Faith: My Journey with God*, will touch your heart and feed your soul with daily offerings of both poignant and personal experiences about family, relationships, internal struggles, journeys of faith and love, and so much more. Each devotional rings of truth and light, even in life's darkest moments, and reminds the reader that hope is but a prayer away. That when we seek to know Jesus and have relationship with Him through all our ups and downs, we will find the way, the truth, and the life we're meant to live." – *Mirachelle Canada*, author, devotional writer, teacher, theatre director

"A must have is how I would describe this book. From encouragement, to comfort, to gentle reminders regarding the importance of spending quality time with God, this book of devotionals offers it all. I thoroughly enjoyed this read." – *Temeka "Positivity Inspires" Borden*, author

"This devotional reveals the openness and vulnerability that every Christian should experience on their journey with God. It's a must read!" – *Joesy Pineda*, pastor, counselor, teacher

"Alexis A. Goring takes us through a journey of faith. She shares her journey with every reader and after each devotion, she challenges us to reflect. Each thought helps individuals look deeper into their relationship with God as they navigate through their own journey. Her words will inspire one to dig deeper with Jesus Christ." – *Paul Graham*, pastor and evangelist

"Heartwarming, practical and transformative. Your life will not be the same after reading this book."
– *Kelvin L. Mitchell*, life strategist

Acknowledgments

First and foremost, I want to thank God for inspiring me with the idea for this devotional book. He gave me the gift of writing and for that blessing, I'm eternally grateful.

Thank you to my Mom and Dad for believing in my dreams to write, edit, and publish books that I believe God places on my heart. Your support means a lot to me.

Thank you to all of my family members who are there for me. I appreciate your support and hope that God uses this devotional book to bless you.

Thank you to my dear author friends who are always there for me as we embark on this publishing journey together and support each other as our "book babies" are born.

Thank you to everyone who wrote an endorsement for my devotional book. You are unique, wonderful and valued. I appreciate your kind words and support.

Thank you to my church family who cover me with prayer. You all are the best!

Thank you to all of my pastors from over the years. You are a blessing from God!

Finally, thank you to my book readers. I hope that this devotional book will bless your heart, soothe your soul, encourage your mind and strengthen your God-given spirit.

Table of Contents

Week 1
   God's Family: A Forever Place to Belong   1

Week 2
   Always Welcome   5

Week 3
   God As Our Guide   9

Week 4
   A God Who Hears   13

Week 5
   Jesus is Here   17

Week 6
   BE The Message   21

Week 7
   Our Greatest Resource   27

Week 8
   Making Room for God   31

Week 9
   Silver Platter Faith   35

Week 10
   Knowing Jesus   39

Week 11
   Kings and Kingdoms   43

Week 12
   Hope for a Broken World   47

Week 13
Out of Darkness and Into the Light ... 51

Week 14
The Greatest Countdown ... 55

Week 15
Spartans and Soldiers for Christ: Be A Finisher ... 59

Week 16
A Masterpiece in the Making ... 63

Week 17
Strength for the Journey ... 67

Week 18
God's Hand ... 71

Week 19
Made in His Image ... 75

Week 20
Respect and the God who deserves it ... 79

Week 21
Friends in High Places: My Reflections
inspired by the song ... 83

Week 22
Words of Life ... 87

Week 23
Influencers for Christ ... 91

Week 24
Acknowledgements from God in the Lamb's
Book of Life ... 95

Week 25
God Knows Your Name ... 99

Week 26 Wearing God's Name	103
Week 27 Sabbath Rest	107
Week 28 God's Protection	111
Week 29 The Christian Life	115
Week 30 What's Your Motivation?	119
Week 31 A Happily Ever After that Never Ends	123
Week 32 Enduring Love	127
Week 33 A Different Kind of Overwhelmed	131
Week 34 Our Forever Friend	135
Week 35 God's Not Going Anywhere	139
Week 36 God's Nudge	143
Week 37 Before I Call	147
Week 38 On the Clock God	151
Week 39 Shelter in the Rain	155

Week 40 The Rich Life	159
Week 41 Eternal Awards	163
Week 42 Glimpses of Heaven	167
Week 43 End of Story	171
Week 44 Trusting God	175
Week 45 God's Waiting Room	179
Week 46 The Wait is Over	183
Week 47 Melody at Midnight	187
Week 48 Perfect Christians	191
Week 49 Not My Home	195
Week 50 Preparing for Heaven	199
Week 51 God's Gift: Paid in Full	203
Week 52 The Gathering	207
Author Bio	211
Song Directory	213

Week 1

God's Family: A Forever Place to Belong

> "Yet to all who did receive him, to those who believed in his name, he gave the right to become children of God — children born not of natural descent, nor of human decision or a husband's will, but born of God."
> – John 1:12-13 (NIV)

We all want to belong.

Sororities and fraternities are a big deal for college students in the United States of America. There's a whole grueling, sometimes embarrassing process that young men and women go through just to belong to one.

People go to great lengths and do all sorts of things (good and bad) just to get in because they want to belong to a support system that's like family consisting of their peers.

But what they fail to realize is that they are already invited to be part of God's Family where they truly belong and are loved unconditionally.

Best of all, God's Family is for *life* not only on this Earth but *forever*.

Beth Moore said something in her book *Breaking Free* that resonates with me. She wrote, "God is not only the answer to a thousand needs, He is the answer to a thousand wants. He is the fulfillment of our chief desire in all of life. For whether or not we've ever recognized it, what we desire is unfailing love."

Unfailing love can only come from the heart of God. Not sororities. Not fraternities. Not gangs. Not high school cliques. Not memberships to prestigious organizations. *Only God.*

I love the song "Your Love Never Fails" by Chris Quilala and Jesus Culture. It's about how God's love never fails or gives up on us. He is our Creator, Lord, Savior, Redeemer and truest Best Friend. He loves us with all of His divine heart and He wants us to love Him too. But He will never *make* us love Him because He wants us to love Him out of the *free will* that He gave us, not because we're scared of going to hell or have ulterior motives about making it into Heaven.

God *is* love. He embodies the word and His love for His creation is present in nature all around this world! He is our Heavenly Father and when we accept His Son Jesus Christ into our lives, we become a permanent part of His forever family!

The best part is that we don't have to do anything drastic to belong to God's Family. We just have to trust Him, believe in Him and accept the *free* gift of salvation that He offers humankind through His Son Jesus Christ. According to John 1:12 (ESV), this is how we become part of God's family after we accept Jesus Christ into our hearts: "But to all who did receive him, who believed in his name, he gave the right to become children of God."

It's simple. No strings attached. Only hope eternal knowing that when our life here on Earth ends that we have the promise of spending eternity with Him when Jesus Christ returns to Earth again to take His faithful followers to Heaven.

God's Family is global. When you join His forever family, you gain brothers and sisters in Christ from around the world. Just think how grand our big, diverse family reunion with our brothers and sisters in Christ will be when we make it to Heaven!

Belonging to God's Family is something we should all seek before seeking acceptance from any social or prestigious organization here on Earth. Remember, your worth does not come from what your fellow man thinks of you. Your worth comes from God! Focus on what *He* says about you. Believe what *He* knows is true about you. Let *Him* be your mirror. Listen to His Truth. Don't allow what mankind says to define you, good or bad. Let your sense of self – your core identity – come from God! He thinks you're amazing because He made you. As one of His children, you are loved!

Yes, I know that as mortals, even when we have the Creator of the Universe lavishing His divine love upon us, we still may want to seek acceptance from sororities, fraternities or other prestigious organizations that are *safe* (gangs and cliques are *not* safe). I'm not saying to not seek after those things. I'm just saying to keep God as your primary focus and seek Him *first*. Find out what *He* wants you to do and ask Him for wisdom to make good decisions that will *help* you, not *hurt* you. Also, as you journey through life, remember *who* you are (your identity as a follower of Jesus Christ) and *whose* you are (you belong to God) and refuse to let the opinions of people deter you from remaining a part of God's Family.

In closing, I'd like to share a prayer from Beth Moore about unfailing love that is from her book, *Breaking Free*. She wrote, "Oh, God, awake our souls to see—You are what we want, not just what we need. Yes, our life's protection, but also our heart's affection. Yes, our soul's salvation, but also our heart's exhilaration. Unfailing love. A love that will not let me go!"

God's Love for you will never let you go. Stay close to Him and allow Him to direct your destiny. Remember, *you* are loved and part of His family!

I'd like for you to listen to this sweet song by Tommy Walker. The song is called "God's Family." The lyrics reinforce the fact that you will always belong in God's family. It is a safe place that's filled with his grace and love. You are precious to Him!

~*~

Reflection Questions:
1. What have you done (good or bad) to belong?
2. How does it feel to know that you belong in God's Family?

Week 2

Always Welcome

> "Let us then approach God's throne of grace with confidence, so that we may receive mercy and find grace to help us in our time of need."
> – Hebrews 4:16 (NIV)

Have you ever been scared of wearing out your welcome?

I've been there.

God has blessed me with wonderful friends and family who care about me and want to be there for me. However, I am scared to "wear out my welcome" with these people—as wonderful as they may be—so I keep most of my issues to myself. But lately, God's impressed it on my heart and mind this devotional thought—that with Him, I am always welcome.

Neither you nor I can wear out our welcome when we go to God. He created you so He cares about everything that happens to you...*everything*.

In fact, God wants us to come to Him with our requests! Hebrews 4:16 (NIV) says, "Let us then approach God's throne of grace with confidence, so that we may receive mercy and find grace to help us in our time of need."

There's a beautiful song by CeCe Winans called "Throne Room" that sounds like an invitation to go to God's Throne Room through prayer. The lyrics paint a picture of a majestic yet warm and inviting place that is sacred, holy and filled with the Light of God's presence. The song reminds us to give God his due honor, respect and reverence. She encourages us to cry out that He is holy and Almighty. We are to not just go to God with our requests but we are to worship Him, as the Bible says, in spirit and truth (John 4:24). Ultimately, we are to remember that we are always welcome in His Throne Room.

God is always there for us. Sometimes, He places His people in our lives who are also willing to be there for us and encourage us to remember Him. I thank God for the wonderful people He's placed in my life who are open to being there for me. My brother has said it's never too late to call him. My Mom is always there for me even if some of my issues are on repeat. One of my dear friends who is a prayer warrior said I can text her anytime and one of my church friends told me that it's never TMI because they love me and want to support me.

But still, I realize that they're human as I am and we as humans can get weary of trying to help someone work through their issues. So I never tell them everything, which is wise because the only person who will never fail you is God.

However, I do realize that having my walls up high keeps out hurt but also keeps out love (as a life coach advised me). So I'm working on trying to be more open with the people in my life who care about me. I realized years ago that I'll never know who can be there for me if I never give them a chance to be there for me.

Most importantly, I realize that God, our Heavenly Father, cares about each and every one of His creation. He loves you and me with a fierce passion. He has endless resources and ways to help us with anything that we may face in this life here on Earth.

Best of all, God is available 24/7/365 for all of eternity. He never sleeps! He's always awake and working to make all things work together for the good of those who love Him (Romans 8:28). And He's patient with those who do not love Him or know Him because He wants us *all* to be saved!

So, I'd like to encourage you today to yes, go to the people in your life who care about you and can help you with whatever you're facing but first and foremost, go to God. Ask Him to help you and ask Him to place the people in your life who He wants to help you.

And never, ever, think that God gets tired of your prayers. Pray to Him about *everything*—your joys, your fears, your hopes, your dreams and yes, your problems. Pray to Him any time of the day or night! He's always available and ready to help you. Best of all, you can never wear out your welcome because with God you are *always welcome*.

~*~

Reflection Questions:
1. How does it feel to know that the King of the Universe welcomes you to His throne room and He's willing to hear you and help you?
2. How does it make you feel to know that with God, you are always welcome?

Week 3

God As Our Guide

"Your word is a lamp to guide my feet and a light for my path."
– Psalm 119:105 (NLT)

My Mom discovered a new restaurant and wanted us to try it. So she took the family there. The first time that we traveled there in her car, we became lost on the way but perfectly navigated ourselves back home after dining. This devotional "God As Our Guide" is inspired by our journey home after our second visit to the restaurant.

On the way home, my Mom took a different exit than last time. This exit put us on a road that made the journey home longer than usual. At first, I did not recognize the road. But my Mom—a well-travelled woman—was confident. Keeping her eyes on the road, she spoke words of assurance to me. "You haven't been this way before, have you?" she said. "I have and know where I'm going. It's going to be okay."

Immediately, an idea for this devotional struck me because I realized the spiritual parallel of my Mom's words that are applicable to our faith walk with God. Her words also reminded me of this song by Brian & Jenn Johnson, "You're Gonna Be Okay."

The song lyrics talk about taking life day by day, moment by moment as you press through the dark times and challenging times. It's about trusting God because with Him on your side, you're going to be okay. The lyrics to this song encourage the listener, telling you that you're stronger than you think. The lyrics place emphasis on the importance of holding on to your faith in God no matter what life throws at you.

But back to my realization…

I realized that when the journey through life gets long and the road ahead looks dark and we don't know where we are going or we're afraid of what's up ahead, we can rest assured that we have a Guide who has been this way before and He knows where we're going. Our Guide is Jesus Christ. He spent 33 years walking alongside us on this planet Earth and He knows how to get us from Earth to Heaven. We just need to follow His lead.

The Bible says in Hebrews 4:15 that Jesus was tempted in every way that we were and there is no temptation that He has not experienced but unlike us, He did not sin. This not only made Him the perfect sacrifice "Lamb of God" (John 1:29) who died for our sins then rose again and lives as our High Priest in Heaven; it also makes Him our perfect guide throughout our journey here on Earth.

God knows that we cannot save ourselves; that is why He sent a Savior. The Savior (Jesus Christ) knew He would have to come to Earth born as a baby and grow up on this planet to experience everything that we go through so that He could most effectively guide us and encourage us in our journey. We cannot say that He doesn't understand what we're going through because He's been here and He knows what it's like to experience life on Earth as a human.

Truth be told, life is not easy and the journey can become filled with trials, tribulations, roadblocks, disasters and all sorts of mayhem. But we have Jesus as our Savior and Guide! So let's look to Him for help. He's always there, on our side, waiting and willing to help us survive.

There's nothing that we cannot do with Jesus on our side! So when the road gets dark and you cannot see what's next, ask Jesus to shine His Light on your path (Psalm 119:105). Just like my Mom spoke words of comfort to me, assuring me that we would arrive home safely without getting lost, Jesus spoke words of comfort for us promising that with Him as our Guide, we will arrive home in Heaven safely when He returns to take us there. He said (in John 16:33), "I have told you these things, so that in me you may have peace. In this world you will have trouble. But take heart! I have overcome the world."

Be encouraged, friends, and remember to look to God as your Guide.

~*~

Reflection Questions:
1. How often do you look to God as your Guide?
2. How do you feel knowing that Jesus Christ can save your life?

Week 4

A God Who Hears

"Is anyone crying for help? God is listening, ready to rescue you."
– Psalm 34:17 (MSG)

The idea for this devotional struck me when I interviewed for a part-time position at a daycare. This daycare was for children as young as six months until about Pre-K.

I remember that part of the interview process was to have me observe a classroom to give me a real taste of what working there would be like.

They placed me in the quietest classroom. But the teacher in that classroom told me that it was only quiet because the children were sleeping.

We sat at a table in the middle of the classroom. The adorable toddlers surrounded us, sleeping peacefully on their blue and red mats. They looked like little, sweet cherubs. The teacher of this classroom and I spoke in soft tones as not to wake the children. She informed me about the tasks that she and her classroom aide were responsible for each day and then she said something that still stays with me today.

"I couldn't work in that classroom," she said, pointing down the hall to the Cradle Roll, which was where the noise I noticed from the moment when I entered the secure hallway near the classrooms, originated.

"Really? Why?" I asked.

"Because those babies cry all day!"

We shared a quiet laugh (so not to wake the children in her classroom).

As I walked away from my hour spent interviewing and observing at that daycare, the humor stuck with me and I smiled, but then realization hit me.

I realized that no matter how much we cry – in joy, in despair, in anxiety or what have you – we have a God who hears! Not only does He *hear* our cries, he *never tires* of hearing us cry. He *wants* us to cry out to Him. He is completely invested in caring for us and meeting our every need. We can *never* wear God out! He *never* gets tired of taking care of us! The Bible says that He never sleeps! The Bible says in Psalm 121:4 (MSG):

"He won't let you stumble, your Guardian God won't fall asleep. Not on your life! Israel's Guardian will never doze or sleep."

God never gets tired listening to our cries even if they are *constant* and *never* stop. His patience, perseverance and kindness in caring for us reminds me of the song by Scott Krippayne, "Every Single Tear."

Here is my paraphrase of that song: We may feel like we're not that important. We may feel invisible like nobody knows our name. But we're priceless to God. He sees us and *He* knows each of our names! He sees *every single tear* that we shed on any given day, noon or night. His empathy is unique because *He* feels *everything that we feel*. God looks past our tears and sees our heart. He gets to the core of our pain and as the Master Physician, He carefully and effectively works on us in a way that will heal us and bring about complete restoration. We cry, He cries. But He doesn't just empathize when He hears us cry, He listens to what we cannot even put into words and then He answers the cries of our heart in only ways that He can.

To the world, our cries may be annoying and misunderstood. But to God, our cries draw Him near to us because He's concerned about everything that concerns us! He wants to be there for us and He's readily available to help.

Bottom line: We don't have to face pain alone because we have a God who hears and answers us! The Bible says in Matthew 6:25-26 that if God takes care of the sparrows (He does) then He will take care of us too! The sparrows don't worry about where they're going to sleep or what they're going to eat because they know that their Creator (God) will provide for their every need. The Bible says that we're worth more than sparrows. So we can trust that God will meet all of our needs, from the food that we need to eat to the clothes that we need to wear and to the bills that we need to pay.

Here's how The Message Bible (MSG) words Matthew 6:25-26: "If you decide for God, living a life of God-worship, it follows that you don't fuss about what's on the table at mealtimes or whether the clothes in your closet are in fashion. There is far more to your life than the food you put in your stomach, more to your outer appearance than the clothes you hang on your body. Look at the birds, free and unfettered, not tied down to a job description, careless in the care of God. And you count far more to him than birds."

You are a child of God and He is a Good Father who loves you with *all* of His divine heart. Cry out to God. Pour your heart to Him. Go to Him for help that only He can give. Remember, God is always listening and ready to rescue you!

~*~

Reflection Questions:
1. When was the last time that God meet your needs?
2. How does reflecting on how God met your needs in the past, help you to not fear the future?

Week 5

Jesus is Here

"For I am convinced that neither death nor life, neither angels nor demons, neither the present nor the future, nor any powers, neither height nor depth, nor anything else in all creation, will be able to separate us from the love of God that is in Christ Jesus our Lord."
– Romans 8:38-39 (NIV)

On my walk to work every morning, there is an elderly gentleman who sits in front of a café with a happy smile on his face and a booming voice. Daily, he greets every passerby saying, "Good Morning! Good MORNING!"

His bellowing voice carries behind me as I pass him and continue the two-block walk from the Metro to my workplace. I notice the smiles that his joyfulness puts on people's faces and I cannot help but smile too.

On my way to the metro leaving work on Monday of a week in July 2019, as I waited for the pedestrian light to signal that it was safe to walk across the street, I heard a familiar jingle for WGTS 91.9 FM. So I looked behind me to find the source of the sound. A woman dressed in plain clothes with her hairstyle arranged in neatly groomed locs, was sitting in the man's place from earlier that morning in the same spot that I walked by on my way to work. She looked relaxed and calm as she listened to an old-fashioned boom box that was blaring a familiar song, "O Come to the Altar" by Elevation Worship.

The sound of music and song lyrics resounded over the hustle and bustle that surrounded me. It almost felt like an altar call in the middle of the busy city! Like we were having church on the street. I couldn't help but think that there must be people passing by who need to answer that altar call. People who need hope within the midst of their pain. People who need Jesus (because we all do) to rescue them and help them to survive the trials of life.

Then on the metro ride home that same day, I put down my phone long enough to have a conversation prompted by a young lady who was sitting across from me on the metro. We began talking about work and soon that led to a conversation about going where God guides. When I said how one of my friends often says, "Where God guides, He provides," her eyes lit up and she asked me, "Do you know Jesus?" I replied, "Yes. I do. You?" She said, "Yes!"

We started talking about our faith journey and discovered that we both grew up in Christian homes and made our own decisions to follow Jesus at a young age. We agreed that even when you grow up in a Christian home, you cannot survive on your parents' faith alone; you have to come to know Jesus for yourself: A personal encounter with the King of Kings and Lord of Lords. It looks different for every individual but this same fact remains: It's the start of a beautiful journey, one filled with hope. Life is so much more bearable when you have Jesus going through it with you and keeping you in His care. We parted ways with smiles on our faces. There's nothing like being refreshed by a fellow believer who loves Jesus!

When I returned home that evening, the idea for this devotional struck me and caused me to realize that God had just answered my early morning prayer that I silently whispered to Him only a few weeks ago!

Earlier that July 2019, as I was walking through the city on the way to work, I surveyed my surroundings. I looked up at the office buildings that were towering over my head and making me feel small. I observed the people from different walks of life rushing to and fro, completely caught up in their own little worlds. I saw the tourists who looked awe-struck and happy to be here. My heart went out to the homeless who appeared despondent as they sat on the street corners and lay on benches in the park. As I took in the hustle and bustle that surrounded me, I felt overwhelmed as I realized how easily we can become a society that doesn't have room for God. So I asked God (silently), "Where are you in all of this?"

And then two weeks later, on that very Monday (July 22), He answered.

It's like He was saying: "Alexis. I am here. I am in the homeless man who bellows a jubilant 'Good Morning' greeting to every person who passes by each day. I am on the radio airwaves as Elevation Worship sings a song asking My children who are rushing by to "Come to the Altar." I am riding with you on the metro, reminding you of my love for humankind through your spontaneous fellowship with the Christ-follower sitting next to you. My dear child, I am *everywhere* and I am not going to ever leave you nor forsake you. I am with you wherever you go. You said it yourself when you quoted a dear friend of yours who says, "Where God guides, He provides.""

Then and there, in the quiet of my home as I reflected on my day, I was reminded how Great the Good Lord our God is and how He is with me, always. It kind of reminded me of the song "Here Today" by Scott Krippayne.

If you ever feel like God isn't hearing you or you cannot feel His presence, *trust His Heart* because He loves you. He will never leave you nor forsake you. And He is literally *everywhere*. His Presence can be felt anywhere in the world! The Bible says that if we make our bed in the pit of Hell, He is there and if we ascend to Heaven, He is there! (Psalm 139:7-12). God truly is all around us and He wants to be in our hearts too.

Will you make room for the King of Kings and Lord of Lords? Don't be intimidated by His Majesty. He's a personal God and He wants a *real* relationship with you. That's why He sent His Son Jesus Christ to live on this Earth, show us the way to Him then die and be resurrected to serve as our Bridge from Earth to Heaven. He's our Mediator and Advocate. The Bible says that no one goes to the Father except through Him (John 14:6).

Jesus is alive! And He is here. He is everywhere today, tomorrow and forever!

~*~

Reflection Questions:
1. How does knowing that Jesus is here with you, help you?
2. What can you do to share the love of God with everyone you meet?

Week 6

BE The Message

"Some people are hurting so bad you have to do more than preach a message to them. You have to BE a message to them."

– Joyce Meyer

People. Hurting people. They are everywhere.

The homeless in the parks and on street corners begging for money just to make it through the day ... The child on the school playground who was picked last for the team ... The teen who is bullied by their peers to the point where they consider suicide ... The young adult who is failing out of school ... The middle-aged adult whose career dreams have not come true ... The people around the world who are being persecuted for their faith ... The athlete who has a perfect body but a troubled heart ... The parent who struggles to provide for their child ... The atheist who is facing death.

Pain in this human experience on Earth is inevitable. But what do people do when they are hurting and have no hope? Followers of Jesus Christ know that you always have hope when Jesus is your Savior. But people who do not know Jesus yet live without hope and when life hits them hard, they cannot see the light at the end of the tunnel. This results in despair and sometimes, suicide. But I'm here today to tell you that there *is* hope! His Name is Jesus.

Jesus Christ loves you with his very life! In fact, He thinks you're worth dying for! So He did. The Bible says in John 3:16 (NIV): "For God so loved the world that he gave his one and only Son, that whoever believes in him shall not perish but have eternal life."

But Jesus didn't stay dead in the grave. After three days, He rose to life! He spent time visiting His disciples and followers here on Earth to let them know He is alive and then He went home to Heaven, where to this day, He is our High Priest and Mediator before God. Because of Christ's death and resurrection that completed the plan of salvation for human souls, when God sees a sinner (we humans are all sinners), He sees His Son who died for that person so God doesn't give us the death sentence (Romans 6:23); He gives us grace and mercy. We have a second chance at making it to Heaven thanks to Jesus Christ's sacrifice. Heaven is a truly perfect place that is free of death, pain, sin and sorrow. And that message is hope for a hurting world!

Sometimes, though, hearing a message of hope is not enough. Joyce Meyer said, "Some people are hurting so bad you have to do more than preach a message to them. You have to BE a message to them."

So how do we BE the message of hope for a hurting world?

I cannot speak for every Christ-follower, but for me, I believe that we can be the message by living according to God's Will. The Bible is clear on what God requires of us. According to Micah 6:8 (NIV): "He has shown you, O mortal, what is good. And what does the Lord require of you? To act justly and to love mercy and to walk humbly with your God."

When we act justly, we uplift the poor, we relieve the oppressed and we help to heal the hurting people. When we love mercy, we forgive those who have offended us and share God's grace with those who need it most. When we walk humbly with our God, we put others before ourselves and treat everyone how we want to be treated. Essentially, we *show* the world that Jesus is our Savior and we teach them that He is the only way to Heaven.

According to John 14:6-7 (NIV), Jesus answered, "I am the way and the truth and the life. No one comes to the Father except through me. If you really know me, you will know my Father as well. From now on, you do know him and have seen him."

After Jesus rose from the grave and visited his followers, even they had trouble understanding that He was the way to Heaven. According to my True Identity Bible in a boxed quote that is based on John 14:6-7 and titled, "He Is: The Way and The Truth and The Life," Jesus Christ's disciples had their doubts about how to follow Jesus now that He was going to Heaven. But Jesus, as the Master Teacher, was patient. He didn't preach a sermon; He *showed* them the way. Let's read what this excerpt on page 1539 of my True Identity Bible says:

"Thomas and the others wanted to follow Jesus but didn't know the way he was going. Jesus plainly stated that he is *the way and the truth and the life*. Rather than sermonizing about a complicated set of directions to reach the heavenly Father, Jesus made the way simple: Really know me. When you are lost, would you rather look at a map or follow a person who knows the way? The same is true for coming to Jesus. What an unsaved person needs isn't a complicated explanation but someone to show her *the way* to himself (see also Acts 4:12)."

I like this key point: What an unsaved person needs isn't a complicated explanation but someone to show her *the way* to himself. People who are hurting and don't know Jesus yet need us to, as Joyce Meyer says, "BE the message!" There's a song by Steve Green that really drives my point home. The song is called "People Need the Lord."

Allow me to share my paraphrase of this music message with you.

The music artist (Steve Green) says that he sees people every day with worry in their eyes. He knows that they're experiencing pain that they keep private. He says that they are fearful every day. He hears their silent cries that they cover up with laughter. He knows that sometimes, only Jesus hears their cries and knows the depths of their desperation. But then he gives the listener to his song a call to action! He says that Christ-followers are called to share Christ's Light and God's Word with all of the hurting people in this world. We are to seek the lost and help them find Jesus. We are to show people that Jesus Christ is the way to Heaven and He not only *saves* souls, He also restores broken hearts!

People are literally dying without hope! They are craving something that only God can give. But what they may not know is that Jesus is the hope they seek! God loves them and He is the only one who can truly satisfy their hunger! And it's up to us who follow Jesus and believe in God to show the hurting people that there is hope, that God loves them and that Jesus wants to be their Savior and their Best Friend.

We need to do more than *preach* this message of hope and salvation to the hurting world; we need to BE the message!

The world is waiting for a message that heals their hurting heart. Will you who know Jesus Christ go share this hope, this healing and these words of life with those who need it?

~*~

Reflection Questions:
1. When was the last time you needed someone to BE the message for you?
2. In what ways can you BE the message for hurting people in your life?

Week 7

Our Greatest Resource

"You know how to reach me."

These are the words spoken to me by one of my close friends when I called her in distress but could not put my emotional pain into words.

After two minutes of pauses between starts of sentences and barely-there words on my end of the phone line, that is what she told me before we both hung up the phone.

It comforted my heart to know that she left the door to her support open for me, as she understood that I was not ready to talk about my troubles. It was helpful to know that when I am ready to talk, she will be there.

Thinking back on this experience, a spiritual parallel formed in my mind.

I realized that though this dear friend of mine tried her best to be there for me in my distress, I serve a God who is always there for you and I in our troubling times.

And unlike our family and friends who we may turn to for help, His resources to help us are *unlimited*! He *never* sleeps and He is *always* ready to rescue us. There may be times when we cannot reach our loved ones or a professional for help but we can *always* reach God! He is with us anywhere we go (Joshua 1:9). We are never hidden from Him (Hebrews 4:13). He knows all and sees all (Psalm 139). God cares about *everything* that affects us (Psalm 37:23) and He has *all* of the *resources* we need (Philippians 4:19).

The Bible and several gospel music songs say that our God is the "Balm in Gilead" that is "healing for the soul." Listen to the song "Healing" by Richard Smallwood and his choir as they sing about this great balm that only God can give to us.

God understands the cries of our hearts. Not only does He know what we want to say but are struggling to speak it, He answers us *before* we call (Isaiah 65:24). What a mighty God we serve!

I love God's Heart of compassion and the way that He loves us unconditionally. I am forever grateful that He is always open to being there for us. The Bible says that He has promised to be with us until the "end of the age" (Matthew 28:20) otherwise known as "the end of the world."

I would like to encourage you to run to Jesus Christ (God's Son) when you cannot find the words to say. Go to God when you need help or comfort. Yes, still reach out to the people who God has placed in your life to help you. But never neglect your *greatest* resource (God). He is waiting for you with open arms.

Now the question is, "How can you reach God?"

The answer is simple: Open The Holy Bible and ask God to send His Holy Spirit to guide you as you read. Before you read a word, ask God for understanding and spiritual discernment. Then listen as God speaks to you through His written word. And always *pray*! Prayer is like talking to a friend because God wants to be your friend (John 15:15). Just remember to be respectful, because He is King of the Universe and He is Holy. But don't be afraid to tell Him what is on your heart. God can handle your honesty. Then trust Him to answer all of your prayers according to His will and in His perfect time.

Finally, dear friends, never give up on God because He will not give up on you!

God loves *you* with *all* of His Heart. And just like my dear sister friend told me that I "know how to reach" her, you "know how to reach" God! So don't despair when you are troubled; go to your greatest resource (God). He understands what you are trying to say even when you cannot find the words to say it. And only *He* can *truly* comfort and *heal* your heart.

Be encouraged, dear friends. God's Love for you will never end. I cannot say it enough: Go to God. He is your *greatest* resource!

~*~

Reflection Questions:
1. When was the last time that you went to God first as your greatest resource?
2. How does it feel to know that God's resources to assist you are unlimited?

Week 8

Making Room for God

> "Now as they went on their way, Jesus entered a village. And a woman named Martha welcomed him into her house. And she had a sister called Mary, who sat at the Lord's feet and listened to his teaching. But Martha was distracted with much serving. And she went up to him and said, "Lord, do you not care that my sister has left me to serve alone? Tell her then to help me." But the Lord answered her, "Martha, Martha, you are anxious and troubled about many things, but one thing is necessary. Mary has chosen the good portion, which will not be taken away from her."
>
> – Luke 10:38-42 (NIV)

"*Now* do you have time for me?"

It was that still, small voice that I felt in my spirit and heard in my soul.

Almost like a whisper from God that was only faint because I'd become so busy with the new job that I believed He gave me and my ministry related work that I religiously dove into immediately after returning home from work, that I'd neglected my quiet time with Him.

I am reminded of the Bible story about Mary and Martha. When Jesus came to visit their house, Martha scurried about, staying busy with the hospitality aspects of keeping company while her sister Mary drew close to Jesus, sat at His feet and listened to Him speak.

Feeling like Mary wasn't helping her serve their guest (and growing increasingly upset), Martha complained to Jesus, telling Him to command Mary to help Martha serve Him. But like the kind-hearted and gentle Teacher Jesus always was, He took that teachable moment to show Martha that there is a difference between being busy serving God and actually taking time to get to *know* Him.

What a lesson, not just for Martha but also for *me*!

How often do I become so busy with work, church and ministry-related aspects of my life that by the time I rush through my day and plow through my night serving others and taking care of business, that the next thing I know, I'm asleep, only to wake up the next morning and repeat my life of busyness? The answer for me is *too often*. And God had to let me know that.

My job let me go and once again, I found that now I had much more free time and one of the first things I did was to return to spending more time with Him. What a refreshing experience! As I spent more time with God, I felt closer to Him. As I delved deeper into His Word (The Holy Bible), I became better acquainted with Him. Quiet time with God reaps so many benefits! It helps you to hear Him and receive strength to make it through your day and gives you wisdom to handle anything that you may face.

There is great value to silencing the world and tuning into God. In Psalm 46:10 (NIV), God speaks to us. He says, "Be still, and know that I am God; I will be exalted among the nations, I will be exalted in the earth."

The Creator of the Universe (God) wants to spend time with *you*. He's busy running the galaxies but yet He wants to hear from *you*! God wants you to draw near to Him (James 4:8). Turn off the TV. Silence your cell phone. Take the earphones off your ears and turn your attention from the busyness of your own little world, to the Creator of the *entire* world and *all* that exists!

I'm speaking to myself too because I've been guilty of not making room for God. But I am so grateful that we serve a God who is faithful! He is kind, patient and His love for us endures forever. But that's not a reason to take Him for granted. God does *so much* for us. Can we not make room for Him?

The Bible says in Matthew 6:33 (KJV), "But seek ye first the kingdom of God, and his righteousness; and all these things shall be added unto you."

When we put God first in our life, we make room for Him to *move* in our life! When we make room for God, miracles happen. When we make room for God, He gives His Peace (Isaiah 26:3) as we learn how to trust Him. Making room for God is essential to your everyday life and soul salvation!

The song "Make Room" by Jonathan McReynolds, a gospel music singer, is on the forefront of my mind as I write this devotional. It's a powerful song that will remind you why it's important to spend time alone with God every day.

The lyrics talk about how we make time for what we want in life and we make room for people who (and things that) we treasure. But Jesus Christ needs to be our *first* priority in this life. Nothing else should take His place.

The song is a call to action: Make room for God! Don't just *tell* Jesus that He's your number one, *show* Him! Put Him before Facebook. Check in with Him before you check your social media as you wake up in the morning. Put the phone down, pick up The Holy Bible, open it and allow Him to breathe His words of life into your soul as you spend time searching the Scriptures.

Some Christians like to literally prepare a table for two and talk to God as they sip their coffee and study their Bible. I think that's a great idea if you feel that you need a more tangible way of drawing close to Him.

So dear friends, I admonish *you* and I admonish *me* to please, *make room for God*. Every day that you are in the "Land of the Living" means that He still has a plan and purpose for your life. It's a plan and purpose that you'll only know and be able to carry out if you get to know Him personally!

And how do you get to know God personally? You *make room*.

~*~

Reflection Questions:
1. Are you more like Martha or Mary when it comes to making room for God?
2. How has spending quality time with God helped you?

Week 9

Silver Platter Faith

"Therefore, since we have been justified through faith, we
have peace with God through our Lord Jesus Christ,
through whom we have gained access by faith into this
grace in which we now stand.
And we boast in the hope of the glory of God. Not only so,
but we also glory in our sufferings, because we know that
suffering produces perseverance; perseverance, character;
and character, hope.
And hope does not put us to shame, because God's
love has been poured out into our hearts through the Holy
Spirit, who has been given to us."

– Romans 5:1-5 (NIV)

Ever since I was a youth, I'd prayed to God to give me an unshakable faith in Him that withstands the test of time. When trials and tragedies entered my life, they shook me. But as I aged, I realized that when I asked God for an unshakable faith in Him, He wasn't going to hand it to me on a silver platter. He had to immerse me into situations that would not only test my faith in Him but refine my faith and make it solid as gold.

As the Master Teacher, God knew that He would have to put me in situations that tested my faith in order to produce perseverance and result in that deeply anchored, unshakable faith that I crave.

As Romans 5:3 (NIV) states, "suffering produces perseverance." Sometimes, God needs us to suffer so that we learn how to persevere and hold on to Him. He doesn't send the storms into our lives to destroy us; He sends tough times to strengthen us! He wants us to have a faith deeply rooted in Him and the only way to get that is to go through things. If our life was always easy or as they say "peaches and cream," we wouldn't have faith in God. We may even be led astray thinking that we don't need Him, which is not true because without Him, we would be lost and never make it to Heaven.

There's a song, "The Anchor Holds" and the lyrics speak to the message that I'm trying to convey. Here's my paraphrase of the song, "The Anchor Holds" as performed by Christian recording artist Ray Boltz:

Life's journey can take you through dark nights, making you feel like you're fighting for your life alone while trying not to drown in the open sea. But through it all, God's eyes are watching you and yet the anchor holds! Though your body is battered, though the sails that help you move through life are torn, though you're in the midst of a raging sea, despite the storm your faith in God is anchored deeper than the ocean and you will survive the storms of life because your faith is rooted in Him and He has the power to speak "Peace Be Still" and calm the waves around you. But if He chooses to take you through the storm and not lessen the magnitude of it all, know that you will stay safe as long as you stay in faith with Him.

The song also talks about one's perspective when they're young in their faith and compares their youthful viewpoint to their viewpoint when they're older and more seasoned by life. As a person matures in their faith walk with God, they see that God uses the storms of life to prove His love for you! It is in tough times that we rely on God the most and in those moments, we see how good He is and we learn that no matter what happens, He is in control. We also find it to be true that there's nothing we can do to make Him love us less and there's nothing we can do to make Him love us more because He is our Heavenly Father and He loves us just because we are His creation.

The love of God is a kind, gentle and passionate force that will change you from the moment you experience it and radiate through you for as long as you cultivate your relationship with God. As God's love radiates through you, it will draw people who need Him to you and before you know it, God is using you to change the world for the better with His love.

Beautiful, isn't it?

I hope that you are encouraged to stay strong in Jesus Christ and that you too will ask God to give you a faith that's deeply rooted and withstands the test of time. Trust me, as time moves on and this sin-ridden world gets worse, a faith that's deeply anchored in God is exactly what you need to survive!

~*~

Reflection Questions:
1. What do you do when your faith feels shaken?
2. How often are you working on anchoring your faith in God's Word?

Week 10

Knowing Jesus

"And this is the way to have eternal life—to know you, the only true God, and Jesus Christ, the one you sent to earth."
– John 17:3 (NLT)

A famous entertainer once took a comedic jab at Christians. She mentioned that they think she's going to hell because she "doesn't praise Jesus."

She meant it as a punch line and it drew laughter. But I took her words seriously and it made me sad. I was sad because I realize that it is a trick of the enemy to get people to think that we can save ourselves. He wants us to think that we don't need Jesus Christ, who is the Savior of the world, to save our lives.

The enemy wants us to think that we can get to Heaven by ourselves in any way we want. He wants us to think that we are our own god and our destiny is determined by us. He wants us to think that we don't need God when we have money, health and happiness. He doesn't want us to think about Heaven and what it takes to get there, according to what God says through His Word (The Holy Bible). Most of all, the devil doesn't want us to think that he exists! He likes it when people say that he's a fictional character made up by Christians. Ultimately, what the devil *doesn't* want us to know is that kind of lifestyle will lead us to hell and eternal death.

Why follow the evil one (Satan a.k.a. "the devil") who only comes to "steal, kill and destroy," when Jesus Christ has come so that we may have life and live it "to the full" (John 10:10)?

Why listen to Satan's lies when the Savior of humankind is gently knocking at the door of your heart? Here's the catch: Only *you* can open the door because Jesus is a gentleman who won't force you into having a relationship with Him. He won't force you to choose Him. He won't force you to live for Him and accept His free gift of salvation. But He *does* want you to experience eternal life! Which is why He keeps knocking at the door of your heart.

When I think of the entertainer who doesn't think she needs Jesus, I simply think that's because she doesn't know Him yet. Because to *know* Him is to *love* Him! I can speak from experience. My life "B.C. (Before Christ)" was filled with fear, hurt, anger and a depressed outlook on life. But when Jesus Christ came into my life and I got to know Him personally as my Lord, Savior, Redeemer and Truest Friend, He changed me from the inside out!

God renovated the walls of my heart and restored the broken places. He gave me a new outlook on life, one that's Christ-centered. I began to see the world through lenses of love (Christ's love) and I began to see people as precious souls who are loved by The Creator of the Universe (God). And I had within me, this burning desire to tell the world about Jesus! To show everyone why we all need Him! To this day, I am driven to teach people about Jesus and show them why it's worth following Him. I believe that if that popular entertainer came to know Jesus, she would change her tune and maybe even her career! Imagine the impact she could have for Jesus! I imagine that her millions of fans would become followers of Jesus too because they would see His Love radiating through her and they would want to know the source of her glow.

Knowing Jesus is my greatest blessing in this life! Have you heard the song, "All I Once Held Dear" by Robin Mark?

In the song, the artist talks about how everything he worked so hard to achieve and gain in this life is worthless compared to the blessing and joy of knowing Jesus! He shares that God is his all in all. It is his heart's desire to know God more and to be known as one of God's children here on Earth. He realizes that he cannot work his way or pay his way into Heaven. He knows that the gift of salvation is free and that we are "saved by grace, through faith ... not a result of works, so that no one may boast" (Ephesians 2:8-9).

He often says these words in his song: "I love you, Lord."

Why? Because as I said earlier and various people from songwriters to preachers have declared: To *know* Him is to *love* Him!

In closing, please remember that Jesus loves you and He wants you to know Him. I pray that this devotional today has encouraged your heart and pointed you to the One who loves you with *all* of His heart. I also hope that you will let Jesus into your life (if you haven't already) so that you too may see personally why to *know* Him is to *love* Him!

~*~

Reflection Questions:
1. How does it feel to know that Jesus Christ loves you?
2. What can you do to encourage someone with God's Love?

Week 11

Kings and Kingdoms

"Heaven and earth will pass away, but My words will by no means pass away."
— Matthew 24:35 (NKJV)

It was a normal Saturday morning. Except, I didn't feel like going to church.

I was tired from the week of work and wanted to rest. Another reason why I wanted to stay home was that the weather was too cold for my taste. It felt like the perfect reason to stay home, cozied with a warm blanket and my plush pillow. Sleeping in until the early afternoon sounded good to me.

However, God prompted me to go. Our pastor often says that you're on time for work because they give you a paycheck; why can't you be on time for church because the Creator of the Universe, who enabled you to get that job, wants to meet with you?

So I dragged myself out of bed and began the process of getting ready to go to church. I arrived just in time for the worship service. As I walked in and sat in one of the cushioned chairs, the praise team leader was pausing in her performance to make the congregation really think about the lines in the song they'd been singing as I walked in.

The song was "There's Something About That Name." Growing up, I heard it so many times before but on that Sabbath morning as an adult, it really resonated with me, especially the lyrics that the praise team leader was emphasizing that day. She said, "Listen to this verse: *Kings* and *kingdoms* will all pass away/But there's something about that name!"

Suddenly, everything clicked! I had what educators call a "teachable moment" because I realized that all of my hopes, dreams and plans for my life were what Clay Crosse in his song "I Surrender All," calls "temporary kingdoms on foundations made of sand."

More than that, I realized that all of the most beautiful, wealthy and influential real estate or kingdoms of this world will pass away but the Word of our Lord Jesus Christ and God Himself still stands!

God always existed and He will always continue to exist (Isaiah 43:10)! He cannot be shaken from His Throne nor can His kingdom be destroyed. His authority, sovereignty and endless heart of compassion or humanity will last forever!

No one can kill Him. No one can make Him not be God! He is the Ultimate Authority. The most wonderful Heavenly Father. He is the King of a Kingdom that is good, just, beyond beautiful and will never stop existing!

The Bible says that the streets in Heaven are made of gold (Revelation 21:21)! It also says that the glory of God and Jesus Christ (the Lamb of God), lights the Heavenly City (Revelation 21:23). It also says that there will no more pain, sickness and death in Heaven (Revelation 21:4). And the

Bible also admonishes followers of Jesus Christ to remember that Earth is NOT our home (Hebrews 13:14)!

We are pilgrims passing through this planet (Hebrews 11:13)! So don't get too attached to the kings and kingdoms of this world. Place your trust in God (Psalm 118:8), not mankind. Put your hope in Him!

You can trust God with your very life and soul. After all, God loves you so much that He sent His Son (Jesus Christ) to rescue you from the king of this world (the devil) and give you the opportunity to save your soul (John 3:16) in His Kingdom so that when human history on this Earth ends, you can have hope of an eternity spent with Him.

Yes, we have some pretty impressive and awe-inspiring places here on this planet but none of it compares to what awaits all those who follow Jesus to Heaven! The Bible says that, "Eye hath not seen, nor ear heard, neither have entered into the heart of man, the things which God hath prepared for them that love him" (1 Corinthians 2:9 KJV). All manmade kingdoms and human led establishments will pass away but God's Kingdom will last forever!

Remember these Bible-based truths: God is Good! He is the only true living God. He loves you with all of His Heart and He wants to spend eternity with you! That's why He sent His Son (Jesus Christ) to save your soul. Now all you have to do is to accept Christ into your life, believe in God and follow Him all the way to Heaven.

In closing, I'd like for you to listen to the song, "I Surrender All" by Clay Crosse.

~*~

Reflection Questions:
1. When was your last teachable moment from God?
2. How does knowing that God's Kingdom will never pass away, encourage you?

Week 12

Hope for a Broken World

There's a song that Andrew Peterson leads a choir in singing and it is simply breathtaking! The song is titled, "Is He Worthy?"

Here's my paraphrase of the song lyrics: The world that we live in is broken. It can be very dark but that will never stop God's Light from breaking through! Deep in our hearts, we yearn for our planet to be made new. All of God's Creation is crying out in pain. We need our Creator to rescue us.

But there is *hope* because God already put in place a plan to rescue us from this sin-ridden planet. Read John 3:16. He sent His Son (Jesus Christ) to show us the way to Heaven. Jesus was born as a baby (the Christmas story is real) in the town of Bethlehem (which is located in the Middle East) to a virgin mother named Mary (it was a miracle) who was engaged to marry a kind man named Joseph. Mary raised Jesus and taught him about His true identity as the Son of God. From the start, Jesus loved spending time in His Father's House (the temple or synagogue or what we in the USA call "church"). He was devoted to God, rose early in the morning to not only pray to God but to take time to hear Him and get strength for the journey.

Jesus was on a special mission that only He could accomplish: Put the plan of salvation in place to save the souls of humankind. This meant that Jesus, after His ministry on Earth was complete, had to die. He was crucified on the Cross of Calvary (as Christians call it), which is, according to PBS.org, "a spot outside Jerusalem called Golgotha."

But He didn't stay in the tomb. After three days, He rose again! Read Luke 24 (in The Holy Bible) for the full story. After seeing the people who He loved while he ministered on Earth, He went home to Heaven to see His Father (God) and serve as the Mediator between God and mankind. To this day, Jesus is still serving as our Mediator and Ultimate Advocate! He is our High Priest. The Bible says that He is able to sympathize with everything we go through here on Earth (Hebrews 4:15) because He's been through it too! Only He did not sin.

Best of all, He is coming back to take His faithful followers home to Heaven! When? Only God knows the time (Matthew 24:36). All we need to do is to accept Jesus as our Lord and Savior and then follow Him. The Bible says that as believers in God, we have a "Great Commission" (Matthew 28:16-20) to tell the world about Jesus! It is our duty as Christians to share the Gospel of Jesus Christ with every person we meet.

If you had discovered the cure to cancer, would you keep it to yourself? No! Of course not! You'd tell the scientists, doctors, family, friends, the news media, and the entire world! Why? Because your discovery has the power to save lives!

Followers of Jesus Christ have "discovered" the "Good News" which is the Gospel of Jesus Christ! And in that gospel is the truth that Jesus can save your soul! In that Gospel is the promise of eternity for all who give their life to Christ!

In that Gospel is the message of hope for all the hurting hearts in this broken world! In that Gospel are glimpses of the beauty beyond compare of our Heavenly Home (1 Corinthians 2:9). Best of all, in that Gospel is a roadmap of how to make it from Earth to Heaven (John 14:6). Someone once said that the B.I.B.L.E. (acronym for The Bible) means "Basic Instructions Before Leaving Earth."

There is *so much hope* in the Gospel of Jesus Christ. Won't you share it?

Now let's return to my mention of that song, "Is He Worthy?" by Andrew Peterson and take one more look at my paraphrase of it. I'd like to simply say that only Jesus Christ is "worthy" to save us because He completed His rescue mission when He conquered the grave. He didn't stay dead! He lives! We serve a Risen Savior who is very active in our world today.

Remember that you have Hope! His Name is Jesus (Christ).

Reflection Questions:
1. How does it feel to have hope?
2. Who in your life needs to hear about the Savior of the world?

Week 13

Out of Darkness and Into the Light

"But you are not like that, for you are a chosen people. You are royal priests, a holy nation, God's very own possession. As a result, you can show others the goodness of God, for he called you out of the darkness into his wonderful light."

– 1 Peter 2:9 (NLT)

One summer evening, while riding the Metro on my way home from work, God impressed me with a beautiful thought that I realized is now this devotional!

Here's what happened…

The line that I take home from work starts its journey underground. The train shoots swiftly through dark tunnels illuminated by a few yellow-white lights along the way. Often, the scenery outside the windows of each car on the train isn't too enlightening. All you can see for miles are shades of beige walls of the tunnels and sometimes it's so dark that you can barely see anything.

Sometimes, the darkness that surrounds me while traveling on the train, overwhelms me and makes my mind start drawing parallels to dark seasons of my life and if I'm not careful, I can easily sink into despair.

However, the *good news* is that the darkness on my journey home *doesn't last forever*. No! Why? Because after a few stops, the Metro train that I ride on emerges out of darkness and into the light (the natural light of daytime, with bright, glorious sunshine)! The train is only traveling underground through the darkness for a while but eventually it *does* come into the light (when I'm traveling before sunset).

My point is that in this life, we will have moments (be it mere seconds, challenging minutes, long days and dark nights or many years of trials) where darkness surrounds us and despair tries to grip us. But in those times, we must remember that God is *real* and He is *ever present* with us!

No matter how dark your life may seem, God is still there! He still loves you. He's still watching over you with His Heart of compassion. He's still commanding His Heavenly Angels to minister to you as one of His children who is meant to inherit salvation! (Hebrews 1:14)

The key is to keep moving forward. Keep traveling through the darkness and following the Light of the World. Jesus Christ says in John 8:12 (ESV), "I am the light of the world. Whoever follows me will not walk in darkness, but will have the light of life."

Jesus loves you too much to ever leave you nor will He ever forsake you! He promises this to us in Hebrews 13:5.

I hope that you will always remember this spiritual parallel that God taught me on the ride home that day. He taught me that our journey here on Earth might be filled with dark moments in which we cannot see the light but God promises us in His Word (The Holy Bible) that there is a Light at the end of the tunnel. That Light is Jesus Christ and He promises to not only be there with us in the darkness but He will also usher us into the beautiful light of eternity spent with Him in Heaven where the glory of God lights the city (Revelation

21:23) and there will be no more darkness. I imagine that sacred journey will feel like my metro ride home, emerging out of darkness and into the light! The good news is that journey of being in the light will not be short-lived, it will be *forever* and that my friends, is a *beautiful* truth!

Despite these beautiful lessons that God teaches me, sometimes worry still invades my mind. On the commute home one day, I was worried about my future. It was then that I felt God impress me with these words, "You act like you don't have a God."

I realized that He is 100% right! I should *never* be worried about my future or anything that happens here on Earth because I believe in and serve a God who is Mighty, Sovereign and He has a pure, caring, *forgiving* heart of love for *all* humankind! His love for us is unconditional and eternal, which is why He sent His Son (Jesus Christ) to save us from our sins and deliver us from evil! God wants *all* of His children to be reconciled to Him.

God doesn't want sin to separate us from Him forever! So He made a way through the birth, life, death and resurrection of His only Son to give us a hope that this world cannot give us—hope of an eternity spent free of sin with Him! Read John 3:16-17 for details.

Circling back to my original points: Don't be afraid. Trust God. Keep moving forward in life and remember that if you continue following Jesus Christ, you *will* emerge out of darkness and into the light!

In closing, please listen to this song, "God With Us" by Terrian and allow God to bless you through it!

~*~

Reflection Questions:
1. How does focusing on God's promise to always be with you help when you're going through dark times?
2. When was the last time you thanked God for delivering you?

Week 14

The Greatest Countdown

My friend Abby always does a "Countdown to Spring" every year starting on the first day of the winter season. It helps her hold onto hope of better, warmer weather especially given how brutally cold winters are in the Midwest where she lives.

One night, the idea for this devotional struck me as I thought of a spiritual parallel to this weather-related countdown. I realized that just as when winter approaches and some of us like Abby, start a countdown to warmer spring weather, we as Christians should be "counting down" to The Second Coming of Jesus Christ!

According to Adventist.org, "The second coming of Christ is the blessed hope of the church, the grand climax of the gospel. The Saviour's coming will be literal, personal, visible, and worldwide. When He returns, the righteous dead will be resurrected, and together with the righteous living will be glorified and taken to heaven, but the unrighteous will die. The almost complete fulfillment of most lines of prophecy, together with the present condition of the world, indicates that Christ's coming is near. The time of that event has not been revealed, and we are therefore exhorted to be ready at all times."

The difference is that while we *can* literally count down the days until Spring on our man made calendars, we *cannot* count down the exact days before Christ's Second Coming because The Bible says that "no man knows the hour" (Matthew 24:29-36) of Christ's return to Earth. Only God knows when He is sending His Son (Jesus Christ) to wake up His faithful followers and take them home to Heaven.

Since *no one but God* knows the day and the hour of Christ's soon return, we need to be vigilant and stay sober (1 Peter 5:8). We need to live for God every day by spending time with His Son Jesus Christ (Revelation 3:20) via talking to Him through prayer and studying His Word (The Holy Bible). We need to daily renew our mind (Romans 12:2) so that we can focus on what truly matters and know God's will for our life. Finally, we need to tell the world about Jesus (Matthew 28:16-20) and treat people with kindness (Ephesians 4:32) as we speak the gospel truth in love (Ephesians 4:15).

Just because we cannot do a literal, tangible countdown to Christ's Second Coming does *not* mean that we cannot live for Him as if every day were *the* day that He is coming back to take us home.

This countdown concept reminds me of the church hymn, "We Have This Hope." Wayne Hooper, musical composer, wrote the lyrics for this hymn.

The message within this hymn is about the importance of having hope in your heart that looks forward to the Second Coming of Jesus Christ. It emphasizes how important keeping your faith in God is as you journey through this life. The song is a reminder of greater things to come when Christ returns and takes His faithful followers home to Heaven! It is a reminder that Christ is our Savior, Lord and

King. He loves *all* of His children from around the world and He has great things in store for us in Heaven!

The Bible says, "But as it is written, Eye hath not seen, nor ear heard, neither have entered into the heart of man, the things which God hath prepared for them that love him." (1 Corinthians 2:9 KJV)

Heaven is a beautiful place filled with wonders and gifts to us from God that mere mortal minds can barely begin to imagine! God wants all to be saved and make it to Heaven. So please do not let the distractions and attractions here on Earth stop you from walking the "straight and narrow" (Matthew 7:14) path that leads to your eternal home in Heaven.

Stay connected to Jesus Christ and get to know Him better through Bible study and prayer. Remember, the Bible says that if we draw near to God, He will draw near to us (James 4:8). God loves you with all of His heart! Remember that Bible-based truth.

Keep praying. *Keep* believing. *Keep* hope alive! God *will* send His Son Jesus Christ to rescue us from the woes of this world, *right on time*!

~*~

Reflection Questions:
1. What do you look forward to the most about Heaven?
2. What can you do today to clear away the distractions and focus on your faith journey with Jesus Christ?

Week 15

Spartans and Soldiers for Christ: Be A Finisher

"Therefore, since we are surrounded by so great a cloud of witnesses, let us also lay aside every weight, and sin which clings so closely, and let us run with endurance the race that is set before us, looking to Jesus, the founder and perfecter of our faith, who for the joy that was set before him endured the cross, despising the shame, and is seated at the right hand of the throne of God."
– Hebrews 12:1-2 (ESV)

Imagine. You're about to start a race. Oh, but wait. To even get to the starting line, you must first jump over a wall!

The shot is off now and you must go! Sprint one mile through the woods then hurdle through more obstacles every quarter of a mile. These obstacles include crawling under barbed wire that stretches the entire half length of a football field, carrying a 30 to 60 pound bucket of rocks for a quarter mile up and down a hill and then finishing the race by jumping over a fire pit.

Sound fictional? It's not. This race is real and it has a name, "The Spartan Sprint." It's one of several intense Reebok Spartan Race experiences that participants can run.

My brother ran the race in August 2016. He said that he wanted to "put his fitness to the test." He finished the race in about three hours. He said that the race was taxing but there was nothing like the euphoria of finishing it.

Sometimes when I'm about to work out, a friend or family member will say, "Do some for me." I know that they are just being funny but it made me think of a parallel. Often, we as humans think that something will simply "happen" for us without too much effort on our part. A prime example of this struggle is in regards to weight loss and physical fitness.

We all want to be in great shape, toned and healthy. But how many of us are willing to discipline ourselves, daily, to meet our health and fitness goals? The gym can be intimidating and we can be unmotivated to work out. But if you want results, you need to put in the work. Your dream body isn't going to simply "happen" one day. You've got to work for it.

On the journey to your goals, there will be obstacles and situations that make you fearful. But that's where faith comes in. Pastor Steven Furtick says this in his motivational video, "I Can Handle It": "I can't afford to stay afraid or let my faith hesitate. My purpose is at stake and He who called me is faithful. His strength in me is greater than any pain I feel or enemy I face."

Just like a healthy body doesn't happen without effort, followers of Jesus Christ know that we must put in the effort to persevere through the trials of life and reach that finish line. This is what we must work on in our faith walk with God.

The good news is that we are not alone in our struggles. God is with us and we can do *all* things through His Son Jesus Christ who strengthens us (Philippians 4:13). There is power in perseverance. Pastor Steven Furtick goes on to say, "If I don't stop short, if I won't sell out, it will happen by faith. But faith doesn't take the fear away; it teaches me to fight it. So bring the battle, I'm ready now. I got something for Goliath. I can handle it!"

The Spartan Race is filled with real obstacles that can be intimidating and feel impossible to overcome for the average person. But a true Spartan perseveres and finishes the race, claiming the victory, which is a medal that states they are a "Finisher." Many people that I know wear that silver medal proudly because they are proud of being a finisher of the Spartan Race. It is a victory that is no easy feat.

It's the same for Christians who are soldiers for Jesus Christ. Christians must persevere through trials and trust God to help them get through life. It is no easy feat to follow Jesus. But with God, *all* things are possible.

My brother is a Spartan Race Finisher *and* a soldier for Christ. He said something about his experience in the Spartan Sprint that drives my point of this devotional home:

> "At the end of the day, it's a choice you make to run the race. Nobody can do it for you."
>
> – Trevor W. Goring, PT, DPT

So, dear friends, run your race. Persevere. Keep the faith and finish the race.

~*~

Reflection Questions:
1. Have you ever felt like you cannot handle the hurdles of life?
2. How does your faith in God encourage you to persevere?

Week 16

A Masterpiece in the Making

"God takes the **broken** pieces that Satan leaves behind and makes *masterpieces*!"
– Pastor Pranitha Fielder

Shattered. Broken. Devastated.

We've all been there or will be there at one point in our lifetime. If you manage to go through life without ever experiencing pain then that is not normal. Just like a character said in the movie "The Shack," if you're looking for a pain-free life, you're not going to find one.

We live in a pain-filled world because it is a sin-filled world, which results in pain, heartbreak, devastation and despair entering our life stories.

No one escapes this life on Earth without some form of pain. It happens to you at least once in your lifetime—whether it is a broken arm or a broken heart, you *will* experience pain.

So when you experience pain, what can you do? You can turn to your Creator (God) and ask Him to help you get through the tough times. He can soothe your broken mind, repair your heart, and restore your life. If it's a physical or emotional pain, He can work through others for your benefit.

People like counselors, doctors, first responders, physical therapists, etc. are here on Earth to help you heal.

Recently, I was talking to someone and they told me that nobody's perfect, we all have something to work on. Before she could continue speaking, the title of this devotional "A Masterpiece in the Making" downloaded into my mind and I had to end the phone conversation immediately and start writing this devotional because I realized that God just downloaded inspiration to my brain and He never wants me to keep His messages to myself. So here I am, writing this message to you in hope of encouraging your heart!

I titled this devotional "A Masterpiece in the Making" because if you are a human on planet Earth and you've decided to follow Jesus Christ then you my dear friend, *are* a *masterpiece in the making*!

I want to encourage you to not give up when pain or problems enter your life. But instead, turn to God. He is in control and He will help you.

Did you know that God truly believes that *you* are His *masterpiece*? He clearly states that truth in the Bible. Here's the verse in Ephesians 2:10 (NLT): "For we are God's masterpiece. He has created us anew in Christ Jesus, so we can do the good things he planned for us long ago."

So now that you know that *you* are God's special creation, His masterpiece, embrace this truth and be encouraged! God will never ever leave you. He loves you too much to leave you broken, shattered and devastated. He only wants to lift you up and save your soul. He loves you with *all* of His divine heart!

If you're a perfectionist like me, then you may worry over things or situations in your life that are far from perfect. I'm here to tell you today to let go and let God. Trust Him to work with you on the areas in your life that need improvement. Trust Him to work it all together for your good (Romans 8:28). Allow God to make you into the original masterpiece that He knew you were before you even were aware of it. God knows how to look at rubble and see a diamond. But He does more than see your potential; He helps you to grow into it, which is why all who follow Christ are a masterpiece in the making!

Remember, when God starts making a masterpiece, he carries it to completion just like He promises in Philippians 1:6. This Bible verse promise reminds me of Steve Green's song "He Who Began A Good Work in You."

The song lyrics talk about how when God starts a work within you, He will faithfully complete it. God sees where you are and patiently takes you to where He knows you need to be. The message reminds the listener that when the struggles of life threaten to replace your hope, keep holding on to God and trusting Him because he will see you through!

You always have hope because God is always in the picture, watching out for you.

I hope that you are encouraged by this devotional. May God bless your dear heart!

Always remember that He loves you and He will never leave you (Hebrews 13:5) and that *you*, my dear friend, are His masterpiece!

~*~

Reflection Questions:
1. How does knowing that you are God's Masterpiece encourage you?
2. Next time you feel impatient with the process God is taking you through, what can you do to relax and let Him lead?

Week 17

Strength for the Journey

> "Why, my soul, are you downcast? Why so disturbed within me? Put your hope in God, for I will yet praise him, my Savior and my God."
>
> – Psalm 42:5 (NIV)

One bright and sunny morning, I woke up with my issues on my mind.

As the minutes of what was otherwise a beautiful morning, ticked by, I felt more upset and depressed.

I opened my True Identity Bible and prayed to God, asking Him to be with me as I read the texts. At first, I couldn't focus. So I was honest with God, telling Him what was on my mind. Then I returned my focus to Bible study. And then I saw it: My handwritten, blue ink colored note in the margin of a page in my Bible where I commented on the boxed text. Previously, I had written, "beautiful thought, could be a devotional!"

Inspired, I closed my Bible and asked God to guide me as I turned that thought into a devotional. Less than an hour later, I had written a devotional about how believers in God need to *show* people Jesus Christ, not just preach about Him.

After I finished editing my devotional, I realized that I felt so much better. The heaviness on my heart and sadness in my mind were lifted. I felt refreshed. And I knew why: Instead of reaching out to a friend or family member as I had so many times before, I went straight to my Lord and Savior Jesus Christ.

There's a beautiful song by Byron Cage called "There is A Name." The song basically says that the precious name of Jesus brings healing. It is a holy Name that we are to praise and revere. And what really stands out to me is a practical application he makes toward the end his song when he stops singing and starts preaching. He says:

"You can't really get the victory until you call on the name of Jesus. You can talk to your girlfriend on the phone all night long. You can talk to your mother and to your father, but it's not until you call the name of Jesus that demons have got to tremble. You can cry about it, you can talk about it but until you open up your mouth and begin to bless the name of Jesus and begin to rebuke the adversary in the name of Jesus: I speak healing in my body, in the name of Jesus. I speak deliverance in my spirit, in the name of Jesus! I speak peace in my mind, in the name of Jesus! It's in the Name of Jesus!"

Finally, not only did I learn my lesson of going to God before you go to people; I also experienced the peace and freedom that results in consulting God first! Taking my concerns to Jesus Christ before speaking to anyone else has greatly blessed me.

I am encouraged to, from now on, go to God first.

Just like the preaching at the end of the song says: You can talk to anyone here on Earth but complete and true deliverance doesn't come until you talk to God! Calling on the Name of Jesus sets you free. His name brings healing.

His name brings peace. Only Jesus truly understands you and only He knows what's on your heart before you find your voice to express it.

The older I become, the more I realize what a blessing it is to have Jesus as my Savior and my Best Friend. He understands me completely and sees my flaws yet He loves me unconditionally.

Growing up, I wanted what people called a "forever friend" who was loyal and true and whom I could call upon any time of the day or night. As an adult, when God blessed me with a few forever friends, including one who said I can text her "anytime" as often as I need to. She assured me that I'm "not exasperating" her at all. God also blessed me with a few other God-fearing, true friends who share her sentiment and want to be there for me. I treasure their friendship, kind words and prayer support.

However, I realized that though I am grateful to have true friends who want to be there for me any time of the day or night, the only one whose love for me is unfailing and whose patience in hearing me endures forever, is Jesus Christ. He is my Forever Friend for life.

Jesus is the only one who has the power to give me a peace that passes all understanding (Philippians 4:7). He is the only one who understands me and knows how to help me before I begin to ask. Even the most helpful humans can become exhausted in dealing with other humans because we're *only human*. But our Heavenly Father (God) and His Son (Jesus Christ) never become exhausted! The Bible says that they never sleep (Psalm 121:2-4) nor do they become exasperated from hearing from us whenever we call, even if it's more than once a day. And as for comfort, they send their Holy Spirit to comfort us in ways that mere mortals (humans) cannot. Read John 14:26.

As an adult, I realized how blessed I've always been to have the Savior of the world Jesus Christ (1 John 4:14) on my side. The Bible says that God formed us and knew us before we were born (Jeremiah 1:5). He knows us more intimately than our mamas who carried us for nine months and gave birth to us. Only He is perfectly capable of helping to meet our every need.

The older I become, the more I realize that I always need to go to God first in order to get strength for my journey through life on this Earth. God places His people on this planet in all professions to help us and He definitely orchestrates friendships and relationships between humans that are a beautiful blessing. However, we should never place any human before Him. And no human should ever be one who we rely on for strength. Just like the song by Byron Cage says, only the Name of Jesus has the power to set us free. Calling on Him is a game changer!

As I close this devotional, I'd like to encourage you to always remember that you have a Friend named Jesus Christ who loves you with His life (John 3:16). Ask Him to be your life coach and best friend. He's already cheering you on because He loves you!

Jesus wants to encourage your heart as you go through the human experience here on Earth. He says to not let your heart be troubled (John 14:1) because He has overcome the world (John 16:33) and He can help you overcome it too!

~*~

Reflection Questions:
1. When troubled, have you tried going to Jesus first, before you talk to anyone else?
2. How do you feel knowing that Jesus is always there for you?

Week 18

God's Hand

> "Don't be afraid, for I am with you.
> Don't be discouraged, for I am your God.
> I will strengthen you and help you.
> I will hold you up with my victorious right hand."
>
> – Isaiah 41:10 (NLT)

There's a term that I learned with a technique that I applied when I was a photography student that still stands out to me years after my college class.

The term is called "dodging and burning." I'll explain it later on but first, for those of you who may not know, let me explain the old standards and practices of photography. Much of today's photography is digital but before it became the standard, photographers developed all of their pictures in what's called a darkroom.

There in the (literal) dark, they meticulously removed the roll of negatives (the film inside their manual cameras on which the pictures were taken) and carefully started the process of developing the negatives into what we see as "prints" or "pictures" today.

The process of developing photos manually in the old-fashioned way takes a lot of patience and skill. If you expose your negatives to the light before they're fully developed then all of your pictures are ruined. Even if you still try to develop the prints, you won't see anything on the film because the bright light (be it fluorescent or natural from the sun) destroyed the photos, which is why photographs needed to be developed carefully in a darkroom. It is literally a dark room with special lights that are only bright enough for you to see what you're doing but not bright enough to ruin your film.

Now here's the part about the term "dodging and burning" and the technique used. First, let's look at the definition of this term. According to Adobe.com, "The Dodge tool and the Burn tool lighten or darken areas of the image. These tools are based on a traditional darkroom technique for regulating exposure on specific areas of a print. Photographers hold back light to lighten an area on the print (dodging) or increase the exposure to darken areas on a print (burning)."

Let's talk about the technique. When Adobe.com says that there is a "Dodge tool" and a "Burn tool" used in this technique, it's referring to digital photography where you edit photos on your computer and use those digital tools to accomplish your vision for the photographs.

But before digital photography became so popular and widely used, photographers in the darkroom used a special light and their own hands to perform the action of dodging and burning a photo.

Years ago, I realized that there is spiritual symbolism and metaphor in this professional practice because, just like the photographer skillfully guides his or her hand over a photo to produce the desired outcome, the Creator of the Universe (God) also uses His Hand to direct our life!

Only God is better than any human photographer and His end results are always the best for us! Maybe not *perfect* because of the state of the world we live in but *perfectly tailored* to fit our lives and lead us to Him, which then ultimately results in us being saved in His Kingdom when we make the choice to accept God's Son (Jesus Christ) and follow Him.

Just like a photographer in the darkroom gently and skillfully moves his or her hands under the special light that hovers over the film in order to either lighten or darken certain areas of the photo they're developing, our Maker (God) has His hand over our life. We only need to be still and trust Him as He uses His hand to shed light on the areas of our life that He wants to work on with us. Sometimes, He may allow the darkness in parts of our life to help us draw close to Him and trust Him to see us through.

We need to trust God to use His Hand over our lives to produce the end result that again, may not be picture perfect in our eyes, but is perfect for the work He's doing within us.

So won't you trust His Hand to move over your life (in fact, it already is), to work out all of the details to not only *sustain* you but to *bless* you?

There's a song by Marvin Sapp called "He Has His Hands On You." The song lyrics basically say that even when uncomfortable things happen to you and don't feel good, you can take solace in the fact that as long as you're in God's hands, everything is going to be okay.

The Bible says that God works out everything for the good of those who love Him (Romans 8:28). So when life hits hard and the storms of life roll in, making it difficult to see a safe end, just lean into God and trust Him to see you through. Remember, God's Hand is on you!

~*~

Reflection Questions:
1. How does it feel to know that God is working out His plan for your life?
2. Think back to a time when you felt God's hand over your life. How did it give you hope?

Week 19

Made in His Image

"So God created mankind in his own image, in the image of God he created them; male and female he created them."
– Genesis 1:27 (NIV)

Tests on Facebook are popular. One of the most popular tests is the one where you submit a picture of your face to the test's program and wait a few seconds before the test results appear and show you which celebrity you most resemble.

Tests like these feed on our innate human desire to be likened to greatness. We want to "reach for the stars," take selfies with our favorite celebrities, shake the hands of popular politicians and become best friends forever. Why do we do this? I believe it's because something within us wants to reach a level of greatness that can only be accomplished by connecting with people who have achieved greatness.

Now whether that "greatness" is in the form of a famous person, a popular clique or a complete stranger who looks like our favorite celebrity, we all have a bit of that desire to want those people in our lives. So we buy the magazines, we watch entertainment news, we dream of getting discovered by a Hollywood agent and being propelled into stardom alongside our favorite famous people. Some of us even go as far as to greatly alter our appearance just so we can resemble someone who the world deems attractive or desirable.

But dearest of hearts, don't you know that you *already are* connected to the *ultimate* form of *greatness* in the *universe*? God is Great and you are made in His image! Let's visit the Creation Story told in Genesis 1:26-27 (NIV). Here you will find just how special you are to our Creator God. The passage reads:

> Then God said, "Let us make mankind in our image, in our likeness, so that they may rule over the fish in the sea and the birds in the sky, over the livestock and all the wild animals, and over all the creatures that move along the ground." So God created mankind in his own image, in the image of God he created them; male and female he created them.

God made humankind in *His* image. Let's delve into what this truth means: God created the entire *universe*. All that lives, breathes and moves was created *by* Him and *for* Him. God is the Author of Creation. He *literally spoke* the world into existence. He created everything here on Earth with the power of His Words. But when God created our first father Adam, He bent down in the soil and molded man, creating Adam *in His image*.

We don't need to continue searching for ways to connect with "great" people in this world. We can stop idolizing our favorite celebrities and "wishing upon a star" that we are lucky enough to meet these great people and make them our best friend forever. God does encourage building communities and we need friends in our life. But when our desire to connect with greatness overrides our desire to connect with our Creator who is the Greatest, we have a problem.

God wants our loyalty and devotion, daily. He's out of this world (literally) but He's also right here, with us. God sent His one and only Son into this world to show us the way to Him (John 3:16). So if we really want to connect with someone, it should be God's Son (Jesus Christ) who is our Mediator, the only bridge between Earth and Heaven (John 14:6).

Remember, even the most personable celebrities may not want to connect with their fans. But our Creator God not only wants to *connect* with His creation, He wants to save us!

There's a song by 4Him called "Measure of A Man." The song talks about the tests that this world will give you. They'll test your I.Q., state statistics, compare you on charts and try to rate your worth. But, the lyrics say, what you're truly worth, human eyes cannot see. The song lyrics challenge you to remember that the true measure of a man (or woman), your true worth is in how God sees you. God knows your heart and He loves you completely. His love for you is not based on how you compare on the charts, the level of your I.Q. or how you measure up to statistics. God made *you* in His *image* so to Him you are perfectly made and priceless. He paid a high price for you (1 Corinthians 7:23). You are His. And His love for you is unconditional.

So next time you're tempted to take one of those "celebrity look-a-like" tests, pause and remember that you already look like someone great—you are made in the image of the Almighty God!

~*~

Reflection Questions:
1. How does it feel to know that you're made in God's image?
2. How will remembering that God loves you unconditionally encourage your heart?

Week 20

Respect and the God who deserves it

"Therefore God has highly exalted him and bestowed on him the name that is above every name, so that at the name of Jesus every knee should bow, in heaven and on earth and under the earth, and every tongue confess that Jesus Christ is Lord, to the glory of God the Father."
– Philippians 2:9-11 (ESV)

There's much to learn when starting a new job, no matter what your career.

As a novice reporter, one day I had an assignment that involved interviewing a person over the phone. This interview subject served in the U.S. Armed Forces.

I still remember her name though we'll change it for privacy purposes: Corporal Callie.

I still recall my mistake: Not addressing her by her military title.

I still remember her response: She demanded respect and would not proceed with the interview until I addressed her by her military title.

I still remember my response: I was embarrassed and a bit scared so I quickly corrected myself and instead of saying "Good day, Callie," I said, "Good day, *Corporal* Callie."

Years later, I reflected on that experience and drew a spiritual parallel: God deserves our utmost respect too. But how often do we disrespect Him by our words and actions?

Despite the disrespect that God endures from His children – those who do know Him and those who do not yet know Him – He is patient with us because He desires that all of us be saved in His Kingdom.

The God of the Universe who created all that exists deserves more respect than we are required to give to Kings and Queens and those in positions of authority in every career on this planet Earth.

Brooklyn Tabernacle Choir performs a song called "What A Beautiful Name." The soloist opens the song with a speech about the power of the name of Jesus Christ. She says how there are many famous names in Hollywood and politics but there is only *one* name (Jesus) that brings life and healing and has resurrecting power! The song lyrics give honor and praise to Jesus, saying that He is the Living Word from the beginning, He loves us, and no other name compares to His. God and His kingdom will reign forever.

My lesson learned: God deserves more than our respect. He deserves our praise! The Bible says that the angels cry "Holy" and worship God day and night, never ceasing to praise Him! Let's read about it in Revelation 4:8-11:

"Holy, holy, holy, is the Lord God Almighty, who was and is and is to come!" And whenever the living creatures give glory and honor and thanks to him who is seated on the throne, who lives forever and ever, the twenty-four elders fall down before him who is seated on the throne and worship him who lives forever and ever. They cast their crowns before the throne, saying, "Worthy are you, our Lord and God, to receive glory and honor and power, for you created all things, and by your will they existed and were created."

Now if the King of the Universe, the God who created everything that exists, the Holy One who is Lord over all receives this kind of respect and reverence from His holy creatures in Heaven who never sinned or turned against him like we as sinful humans who He created have done, how much more should we overflow with gratitude, adoration and praise for the God who saved our souls?

The Bible says in John 3:16-17: "For this is how God loved the world: He gave his one and only Son, so that everyone who believes in him will not perish but have eternal life. God sent his Son into the world not to judge the world, but to save the world through him."

God loves *you* with *all* of His Heart! He's done everything within His power to save us because He wants us to be reconciled to Him. Read 2 Corinthians 5:17-19. Now more than ever, I realize that the least we mere mortals can do is to give Him the respect and honor that He deserves!

God is not a strict authority figure who will not respond to you until you address Him by His Holy Name. No! He loves you unconditionally and is longsuffering with your shortcomings. He won't force you into submission. But His love for you should be enough for you to want to submit to Him. Read James 4:7.

God's love for you is eternal. Read Psalm 136. His love for you spans the ceaseless ages of eternity. He's a good, kind and forgiving Heavenly Father who wants what's best for you. So won't you approach Him with reverence and give Him the respect He deserves?

~*~

Reflection Questions:
1. Do you give God the respect He deserves?
2. Why do you think it's important to respect God?

Week 21

Friends in High Places: My Reflections inspired by the song

"Some trust in chariots and some in horses, but we trust in the name of the Lord our God."

– Psalm 20:7 (NIV)

There's a song that Larnelle Harris, a gospel music artist, sings that inspires me to this day. The song's title is "Friends in High Places." In this song, Harris talks about how he has hope in troubled times, a reason to smile when he's sad, friends who uplift his spirit when he's feeling depressed, and he talks about how they watch over him everywhere he goes.

At first, you might think he's singing about his closest human friends here on Earth. But as the song continues, you find out that he's talking about God the Father, Jesus Christ the Son and The Holy Spirit. He's also talking about God's Angels (Hebrews 1:14) and how his friends are all in high places but yet so close to him in his life experiences.

The first time I heard these lyrics was through the beautiful singing voice of an upperclassman named Porsche during our weekly Chapel program offered through our private, Christian academy (high school). On that day, Porsche provided the special music for the chapel service. The main lyrics of the song stuck with me: "I've got friends in high places."

She was singing about God being our Friend in the Highest Place (Heaven) and speaking to the fact that He has our best interest at heart.

This song returned to my mind several years ago in my adult life, when I worked as a reporter for a newspaper. My former colleague Tiffany, who at the time was new to Journalism, asked me how I'm not nervous when I'm interviewing famous people at city council. She gushed about how they were all like celebrities in high places and wanted to know how I managed to maintain composure and professionalism without being awestruck and speechless.

I told her about that song "Friends in High Places" and reminded her that as believers (because she too was a believer in God), we have the Ultimate Friend in High Places. His name is God and He has our back!

I talked about how knowing this fact helped me to keep things in perspective because we're all humans whether we are famous or not and we all deserve respect. I don't look at it as interviewing a celebrity; I look at it as interviewing a fellow human. I approach each interview with looking them straight in the eye, showing a warm smile and giving them the respect that they deserve.

I don't spend too much time thinking about their status or fame. I just try my best to implement Luke 6:31 (a Bible verse that is also known as "The Golden Rule"), which tells us to treat others how we want to be treated, and I do my best to maintain professionalism in all cases.

The Bible says in Colossians 3:23-24 (NIV), to work like you're working for God, not man. This helps me to remember that we're all mankind, no matter what our status. We all need Jesus! And the beautiful truth is that God wants to be our friend. How remarkable is it that the *Creator* (God) of the *Universe* wants to be *your* friend?

An old church saying goes, "God sits up High (in Heaven) and lives down Low (on Earth)," which means that He did not set this world in motion then leave us to figure out everything for ourselves. No! God created our world and *stayed* in the picture! The Bible says that God is Omnipresent, which means He is *everywhere* at *all times*. He knows everything and sees everything. God cares about everything that affects us and He can handle our honesty, so we shouldn't be afraid to speak to Him about anything!

Another point that the song reminds me of is when we as mere mortals are in trouble here on Earth, we feel comforted when we know that we have "friends in high places" who can take care of us by "pulling the strings" and solving our dilemmas. But even if we have friends in high places here on Earth, we still need to remember that they are *only human* and at the end of the day they can only do so much!

Humans cannot save our souls! Only God can do that through the sacrifice of His Son Jesus Christ. Open The Holy Bible to the Book of John and read about the *free* gift of salvation offered to us all, thanks to Jesus!

Let's not forget our Greatest Friend (God) in the highest of places (Heaven). He is Lord over *all*. May we remember that only Jesus can truly save us!

~*~

Reflection Questions:
1. How does it make you feel to know that Jesus Christ is your greatest friend in the highest of places (Heaven)?
2. How has Jesus intervened in your life?

Week 22

Words of Life

"The tongue has the power of life and death, and those who love it will eat its fruit."

– Proverbs 18:21 (NIV)

An outpouring of love on Facebook a few years ago on my birthday (May 23) inspired this devotional. Family and friends showered me with love through kind words about what they think of me. My Facebook wall was filled with these lovely sentiments that made my heart smile and breathed life into my spirit.

I saved the comments and returned to read those words of life on days that I felt discouraged or moments where I needed encouragement. However, God taught me a valuable lesson pertaining to how I was feeding on words of life from my fellow mere mortals.

Here's what I realized: Words of life from loved ones give you a boost and you can live on those words for days but it does not compare with God's Words of Life spoken over us in The Holy Bible. His Words give *eternal* life.

There's a song performed by Michael W. Smith that resonates with me and shows us the value of soaking in and speaking words of life. The song is called "Ancient Words." The lyrics speak of "ancient words" that refer to the words in written in the Bible more than a thousand years ago. These words may be ancient but the song shows how they are not only still relevant today, but also hold power to transform lives! These words of life come from God's own heart and these words were written by humans who God inspired to write His Word on paper. These words give the reader hope, strength, coping skills and a guide through Earth to Heaven.

Just like families hand down traditions to future generations, God wants us who believe in Him to hand down His Word to everyone. He wants us to share His hope with a dying world to inspire their hearts and help them see that there is hope in the name of Jesus Christ. I like how Smith says you must have an open heart to receive the ancient words that give life.

Just like you cannot receive a blessing with closed fists, you cannot understand God's Word until you ask Him to open your heart to what He wants to teach you. I know from experience that opening my heart to Jesus Christ was the best decision I've made in this life. He filled me with His hope, grace, love, mercy and peace. I've never felt more loved than being loved by my Creator, Redeemer and Savior. "Jesus saves" is more than a religious cliché; it's a beautiful reality!

So, what does God, the Creator of the Universe and all of the worlds, think of us mere mortals?

He loves us and nothing can separate us from His love. – Romans 8:37-39

He made us in His image. – Genesis 1:27

We are His masterpiece. – Ephesians 2:10

We are special to Him. – Deuteronomy 7:6

We are the salt and light of the world. – Matthew 5:13-16

We are adopted into His family (and that makes us royalty)! – Ephesians 1:5

He believes that we're worth dying for! – John 3:16

I hope that after reading those selections from Scripture that you're as convinced as I am that spending time with God and allowing what He thinks of us to matter most in our lives, is what we need to focus on.

I know that I can become too focused on what mere mortals think of me or how print media/social media portrays me. But as I write this devotional, I am reminded once more that what matters most is what *God* thinks of me, how *He* sees me and what *He* wants me to do with this life He's given me.

All forms of media have the power to uplift and inspire. But there are also people who use it to discourage and upset people, which is why it is *so* important to be careful what you spend your time seeing and hearing.

I hope that you will join me in striving to press into God's presence and experience His perfect peace as we work to keep our mindset fixed on Him (Isaiah 26:3) as we endeavor to value *His* words about us over words from our fellow inhabitants in this world. Kind words from loved ones are a good thing to receive, but allowing your mind to soak in wisdom and words of life from God is even better!

In closing, I challenge you to speak words of life over yourself and over your loved ones every day as you point them to the One (God) who speaks Words of Life.

~*~

Reflection Questions:
1. How often do you read The Holy Bible?
2. Have you tried reading and speaking God's Words of Life over yourself?

Week 23

Influencers for Christ

> So we are Christ's ambassadors; God is making his appeal through us. We speak for Christ when we plead, "Come back to God!"
>
> – 2 Corinthians 5:20 (NLT)

Early in March 2015, I was selected to participate on the book launch team for one of my favorite authors, Melissa Tagg. She was looking for people to serve as influencers for her latest book release *From the Start*.

Hundreds of people applied for this position but only around 100 were selected. So when I found out that I was one of those selected, my excitement was uncontainable for three main reasons! Reason #1: I love reading Christian romance books. Reason #2: I love Melissa Tagg's novels. Reason #3: The main character in Melissa's book *From the Start* is a screenwriter of made-for-TV movies and that is one of my ultimate career goals!

Allow me to explain what exactly my role as an influencer is, in Melissa's words:

> "Influencers—aka the enthusiastic readers who help spread the word about an author's book—are *so* treasured."

> "An influencer agrees to say good things about *From the Start* in exchange for a free copy of the book."

> "An influencer agrees to read and review *From the Start* as soon as possible. If you're able to post your review within a month of receiving the book, that's ideal."

As expected, after I read Melissa's book, I delved deep into promotional activities to get the word out about Melissa's book. I did so with great enthusiasm because I believe in the product and when you believe in a product, sharing with the world flows naturally.

So where am I going with this and what does my devotional title, "Influencers for Christ" mean? Okay, are you ready? I'm going to tell you.

Just like believing in the product (Melissa's book) prompted me to become an influencer and tell the entire world about how good this book is and why I love it, I believe God expects the same response from us who believe in Him and accept the gift of salvation offered through His Son Jesus Christ which in turn makes us…you guessed it, *Influencers for Christ*!

Let's see what God's Word (The Holy Bible) says about us as influencers or rather, *ambassadors*, for Jesus Christ. As followers of Jesus Christ and ambassadors for God, we are given the task of "reconciling" people to God.

Let's read about our special task in 2 Corinthians 5:18-20 (NLT): And all of this is a gift from God, who brought us back to himself through Christ. And God has given us this task of reconciling people to him. For God was in Christ, reconciling the world to him, no longer counting people's sins against them. And he gave us this wonderful message of reconciliation. So we are Christ's ambassadors; God is making his appeal through us. We speak for Christ when we plead, "Come back to God!"

What an honor to be an influencer for God's kingdom, an ambassador for our Heavenly Father, an *influencer for Jesus Christ*.

When I found Jesus Christ as my Savior, Redeemer and Friend, He changed my life from the inside out. He created a hunger within me for His Word. As I delved deeper into *God's Book* (The Holy Bible), it was like drinking from a deep well of Living Water because I could not and still cannot, get enough! The more I read about God and learn how to live my life for Him, the more I want to tell the world about the gospel of Jesus Christ!

When you sign up to become an influencer for Christ, you won't have to fill out a form and submit it to a publisher or Public Relations person then hope that they select you to be one of their influencers. No! All you need to do is to accept Jesus as your Savior and ask Him into your heart and then that's it, not only are you on His team as a influencer for Christ, you're unlimited to the many ways that you can tell the world about Him!

Blogs, Facebook and social media are wonderful ways to witness for God. But the most effective way I would say to be an influencer for Jesus Christ is not to simply *tell* the world about the good Lord but to *show* them through your daily living.

When you let Jesus into your heart and make room for Him in your life, He *will* transform you from the inside out. He *will* give you a genuine agape love for His people and He *will* inspire you to go and tell the entire world who God is and show the world your story of how God's glory came into your life and changed you.

The song "I Will Follow Christ" that is sung by Clay Crosse, Bebe Winans & Bob Carlisle resonates with me and shows us how to be influencers for Christ. In the song, the music artists paint a picture of how Jesus Christ's original influencers (known as his 12 Disciples), journeyed through life together. They knew Jesus intimately because they spent most of their time with Him. They witnessed His wonders and miracles firsthand. They were inspired by His ministry and continued following Him even when they didn't understand. They stood firm in the face of persecution because they were determined to follow Jesus Christ all the way to Heaven. But following Jesus and being an influencer for Him didn't stop after Jesus Christ's death and resurrection. He still needs influencers for Him today!

God needs people who believe in Him to show people who don't know Him yet that Jesus Christ is the only way to Heaven. God needs faithful ambassadors to represent His Heavenly kingdom and to share His Hope, the Good News with people who desperately need it (even if they don't know they need it). We are to speak the truth in love (Ephesians 4:15) and stay faithful to the cause of Christ.

Becoming an influencer for Christ is a decision that will change your life forever and impact the world for the better!

~*~

Reflection Questions:
In what ways can you be an influencer for Christ to the people in your life?
Why is it important to "speak the truth in love" to everyone?

Week 24

Acknowledgements from God in the Lamb's Book of Life

> "I tell you the truth, everyone who acknowledges me publicly here on earth, the Son of Man will also acknowledge in the presence of God's angels."
>
> – Luke 12:8 (NLT)

This devotional was inspired one July 2017 summer night. I'd logged into my Facebook page and saw an update form one of my friends. She's an author who's working on a new novel. I'm one of her beta readers.

The message from my author friend noted how she would award her beta readers after her book was ready to be published. She said, "As a reward for being a HUGE part of this creation, you'll have your name mentioned in my acknowledgments and you'll get a free, autographed copy of the paperback when it releases." As I read this note, Luke 12:8 came to mind and a parallel was formed!

I realized that book enthusiasts get excited when their name is mentioned in the acknowledgements of a book by one of their favorite author friends. It's exhilarating that though in most cases we, not an author, played a role in helping the author create this polished book. We like to see our name in print. It gives us a feeling of significance and lets us know that the author wants us in their life.

But did you know that there's a great book that God wrote called The Book of Life? Everyone whose names are written in the Lamb's Book of Life will be saved and go to Heaven when Jesus returns to Earth to take His faithful followers home. Let's read what the Bible says about this book in Revelation 13:8 (NLT): "And all the people who belong to this world worshiped the beast. They are the ones whose names were not written in the Book of Life that belongs to the Lamb who was slaughtered before the world was made."

Let's read more about this in Revelation 21:22-27 (NIV): "I did not see a temple in the city, because the Lord God Almighty and the Lamb are its temple. The city does not need the sun or the moon to shine on it, for the glory of God gives it light, and the Lamb is its lamp. The nations will walk by its light, and the kings of the earth will bring their splendor into it. On no day will its gates ever be shut, for there will be no night there. The glory and honor of the nations will be brought into it. Nothing impure will ever enter it, nor will anyone who does what is shameful or deceitful, but only those whose names are written in the Lamb's book of life."

The Bible also says in 1 Corinthians 2:9 (KJV), "But as it is written, Eye hath not seen, nor ear heard, neither have entered into the heart of man, the things which God hath prepared for them that love him."

Now that is a happily ever after ending that I want for my life story!

Heaven is going to be wonderful. Eternal life free of sin and pain will be worth the struggles we face here on Earth. Most importantly, having our names written in the Lamb's Book of Life brings me so much hope and joy! It shows just how special and significant we are to God and it portrays the enduring, forever love that our Savior Jesus Christ has for humankind.

It's wonderful to have our names mentioned by our favorite authors in the Acknowledgements section of their book but there's one author friend's book that I most want my name to be in and that's in the Lamb's Book of Life. Jesus Christ is the Lamb of God and I want to be acknowledged in His book, don't you?

So what can you do to be acknowledged by God? By committing your life to Him and accepting the free gift of salvation offered to you through the sacrifice of His Son Jesus Christ! Live your daily life in obedience to God. Study the Bible and apply its principles then watch your faith in God grow!

Let's read what Jesus says about how to be acknowledged by God. According to Matthew 10:32-33 (ESV) He said, "So everyone who acknowledges me before men, I also will acknowledge before my Father who is in heaven, but whoever denies me before men, I also will deny before my Father who is in heaven."

In closing, I'd like for you to listen to the song "I Am Not Ashamed" sung by the Heritage Singers. It's a beautiful melody that encourages the listener to not be ashamed of knowing Jesus and sharing "the gospel of Jesus Christ."

Remember, it is better to be acknowledged by God than by man.

~*~

Reflection Questions:
1. How has the gospel of Jesus Christ helped you when you were hurting?
2. In what ways can you share the gospel of Jesus Christ with this world?

Week 25

God Knows Your Name

> "But whoever loves God is known by God."
> – 1 Corinthians 8:3 (NIV)

Pastor Charles A. Tapp shared a story one Sabbath morning, as a sermon illustration for his congregation.

He talked about a time in his life when he was about to graduate from seminary with his M.Div. (Master of Divinity), which is a degree that he needed to be a pastor. Pastor Tapp said that his fellow theology students were gathered around talking about how they know this person and that person who will give them a job when they graduate. Suddenly, they turned to him and asked, "Charles, who do *you* know?" Without skipping a beat, Pastor Tapp replied, "I know God."

Years later, this sermon illustration returned to my mind in relation to my own search for a job in the field in which I studied. I earned a B.A. in Print Journalism and an MFA in Creative Writing. I've trained all of the talents the God gave me through studying for these degrees. But the dream job has not yet materialized. I worked hard for a media organization and loved it but due to budget cuts, I was laid off.

So for a while, I tried to do what a lot of aspiring creative professionals do—reach out the big names in the business. Hoping to connect with the famous ones who have a proven track record of success because as someone told me last year, "Once Oprah knows your name, you're good." And by that they mean that if Oprah knows your name and likes your work, she can open doors and do wonders for your career.

But lately, I am reminded of that sermon illustration and my Mom's advice. My Mom told me, "Why are you trying to network with all of the big names in the industry? Just network with God because He knows everybody."

A song by one of my favorite Contemporary Christian music singers comes to mind. The song is called "He Knows My Name," and Francesca Battistelli sings it.

The essence of the song is that we are less than perfect. We might not choose ourselves to be on a winning team or celebrated as a champion so we think that God should choose somebody else. But God sees our heart. He made us, which means He knows exactly what we need and when we need it. The song points out that you don't need your name in lights because you're already famous in God's eyes and He knows your name.

This song is very comforting to me because it reminds me of what really matters and teaches me that even if my name is never in lights or I get my dream job, I will be more than okay because God knows my name and He will take care of me whether it be by blessing me with my dream job or opening my eyes to something He has planned that's better than what I've imagined.

Ultimately, I realize that God knows my name and He is in control of my destiny. I choose to trust Him to lead me to the job that He knows I need. The older I get, the more

I see that I don't always know what I really need nor do I always know what's best for me. But I am so encouraged to know that God *always* knows exactly what I need and His plans for my life are the best! The Bible says that God will supply all of my needs (Philippians 4:19) and that I can trust Him (Proverbs 3:5-6). I choose to trust God. I want what He wants for my life to be what I receive. I choose to give Him the pen and let Him write my story. After all, God is the best Author (Hebrews 12:2)!

If you're experiencing a similar season in the journey to your dream career, I want to encourage you to reach out to God. He loves you with all of His heart and He will connect you with the right people, place you in the right situations and bless you with what you need and maybe never even knew you wanted.

Reflection Questions:
1. How does it feel to know that God knows *your* name?
2. Have you tried turning to God when you are in need?

Week 26

Wearing God's Name

> "They will see his face, and his name will be on their foreheads."
>
> – Revelation 22:4 (NIV)

God, a beautiful song called "Wear Your Name" and K-LOVE, which is my favorite Christian radio station, inspired this devotional. K-LOVE is based in California and is available online so that music lovers around the world can tune in and hear Christian Contemporary songs.

I love this radio station so much that I decided I wanted everyone around me to know about it. Therefore, I ordered one of their window stickers and plastered it to my car with hope that their wonderful ministry would impact everyone who saw their name on my car. My desire is that when people see my window sticker, they will connect with K-LOVE online and as they use K-LOVE's endless resources then they too would be changed for the better.

Lately, God inspired me with a lesson point based on my desire to wear K-LOVE's name on my car and that lesson is this: Just like how my deep appreciation for K-LOVE inspired me to advertise their name so others would be impacted, so it is with Christians. We should want the world to know about Jesus Christ so much so that we wear His Name and we wear it well. You do not need to plaster or tattoo Jesus Christ's name to your forehead but the world should know that you know and love Him by the way you live your life and by the words you say. They should see Jesus in the way that you treat people especially those who offend you.

So how do we wear God's Name and "wear it well?" The Bible answers this question in Micah 6:8 (NIV) which says, "He has shown you, O mortal, what is good. And what does the LORD require of you? To act justly and to love mercy and to walk humbly with your God." When you live for Jesus and live out His command in Micah 6:8, you are indeed wearing God's Name and wearing it well!

If you'd like a musical illustration of how to wear God's name well, listen to this song "Wear Your Name" by Gylchris Sprauve. In this song, he sings about the urgency and necessity to represent Jesus Christ in these troubled, modern-day times. This song is a call to reject your sinful nature that is fed by the sin in this world and choose to stand for Jesus Christ because you are one of His children and He loves you with His very life!

Sprauve emphasizes the importance of standing for what is right, denying the desires of your flesh, and allowing God's Holy Spirit to direct you into being a good reflection of God's Love to the world.

"Wear Your Name" is a beautiful song with a relevant message.

Sprauve expresses through his song lyrics that now more than ever, Jesus Christ needs His faithful followers to wear his name and wear it well! He needs each of us to be His message of hope and salvation to this hurting and dying world. He needs us to invite Him to live in our hearts so that He can shine through us. He needs us to carry His Good News to the entire world and tell everyone about Him so that everyone may have a chance to accept His free gift of salvation and have the hope of going home to Heaven when He comes again to take His faithful followers home.

We need to stand strong for Jesus no matter what comes our way. We need to be sold out for Jesus every single day. We need to submit ourselves to God and resist the devil so that he will flee from us (James 4:7).

We may have failed to properly represent Jesus Christ and His life-giving message to the world but God will forgive us of all our sins if we only repent and turn away from our sins then do God's will. Ultimately, we need to say "no" to the sinful ways of this world and "yes" to following Jesus all the way to our eternal home (Heaven).

Remember: Earth is not our home. So let's live with a Heavenly focus—one where we shine for Jesus Christ and share His Light with a world that so desperately needs to see Him.

~*~

Reflection Questions:
1. How has Jesus Christ impacted your life?
2. In what ways today can you show someone God's love?

Week 27

Sabbath Rest

"Remember the sabbath day, to keep it holy. Six days shalt thou labour, and do all thy work: But the seventh day is the sabbath of the Lord thy God: in it thou shalt not do any work, thou, nor thy son, nor thy daughter, thy manservant, nor thy maidservant, nor thy cattle, nor thy stranger that is within thy gates: For in six days the Lord made heaven and earth, the sea, and all that in them is, and rested the seventh day: wherefore the Lord blessed the sabbath day, and hallowed it."

– Exodus 20:8-11 (KJV)

Growing up in the church, I didn't always understand this concept of resting once a week, and as an energy-filled youth I didn't always look forward to it. But as I grew up and more demands were placed on my life – especially when I worked a full-time job for five days a week – I started to value and cherish Sabbath rest more deeply.

According to The Bible, God made the world in six days but on the seventh day, He rested. God doesn't need rest because He is a God who never slumbers (Psalm 121:3-4) but He's also a Master Teacher and I believe that He rested on the seventh day (Sabbath) to set an example for humankind as to what we need to do in order to maintain proper balance.

The Bible says that our bodies are "fearfully and wonderfully made" (Psalm 139:14) but if we don't take care of it with proper exercise, nutrition and rest then eventually, we'll either fall apart or become very sick. God knows that we need to take care of our bodies and He knows that we need time to rest from our labor at least once a week. So He created Sabbath.

Sabbath is not meant for us to simply rest and not do anything! We're supposed to spend time with God by going to church and fellowshipping with other believers. We are to worship Him and keep His Sabbath Day holy, which for my faith denomination means we don't work on Sabbath unless we're in the healing career fields (doctors, nurses, etc.) because even Jesus Christ when He was here on Earth, healed people on the Sabbath day (Matthew 12:10-13). However, when it comes to going to sporting events like football games or working our non-healing or emergency service related day job on the Sabbath day, we don't do that. Let's read about that in Isaiah 58:13 (NLT):

> "Keep the Sabbath day holy. Don't pursue your own interests on that day,
> but enjoy the Sabbath and speak of it with delight as the Lord's holy day.
> Honor the Sabbath in everything you do on that day, and don't follow your own desires or talk idly."

God knows we need to rest.

Two examples of why we need to rest and reflect on God's goodness (appreciating all that He does for us) and remember Him as our Creator, once a week come to mind: One from a former colleague and one from a conversation amongst post office workers that I overheard.

When I was a substitute teacher, one of my assignments was for a middle school. I remember a teacher there who said she works "seven days a week." When she's not teaching, she's working her retail job not just on the weekdays but also on the weekends.

Now for those of you who may not know, teaching is a time-consuming job. When I was a teacher, I only had rest on Sabbath hours (from sunset Friday to sunset Saturday). After that sacred time of rest, I had to do school work (lesson planning and grading papers) in order to stay on track and up to date with all of the demands of my work as a teacher. It was overwhelming! And it made me appreciate Sabbath rest on a deeper level. It also gave me empathy for teachers and other professionals who have to work seven days a week in order to stay afloat financially and make ends meet or simply to keep up with the demands of their career.

The other example that comes to mind was when I was waiting in line at a post office. I overheard one of the workers saying how tired she was and how she longed for rest. Then I heard her colleague reply, "You can rest when you die." Ouch. Such a statement is true (The Bible says in Psalm 13:3 that death is like sleeping until Jesus Christ returns to wake you up and take His faithful followers home to Heaven) but that statement from the post office worker must have hurt her colleague who was exhausted by her work!

God never meant us to run ourselves ragged with the demands of life and work which is why in His great wisdom, He made the Sabbath Day for us to rest and reflect on His goodness. I know from experience, especially as an adult now, that keeping God's Sabbath Day holy every week has helped to renew my mind and rejuvenate my soul. I am so much more balanced and happier when I keep His Sabbath every week. I am also more grateful as I reflect on all He's done and continues to do in my life in the lives of others.

A song called "Sabbath Day" is performed by The AsidorS. The lyrics speak to God, thanking Him for loving humankind so much that He created this world and Sabbath rest. They call it the Sabbath Day an "eternal gift" given to us by God. They sing about how special the Sabbath is and how it is important to open that gift from God on the seventh day of every week (Saturday). They even remind the listener of the Bible promise from God found in Isaiah 58:13-14 (NASB), which in the Bible, says:

> "If because of the sabbath, you turn your foot
> From doing your *own* pleasure on My holy day,
> And call the sabbath a delight, the holy *day* of
> the Lord honorable,
> And honor it, desisting from your *own* ways,
> From seeking your *own* pleasure
> And speaking *your own* word,
> Then you will take delight in the Lord,
> And I will make you ride on the heights of the earth;
> And I will feed you *with* the heritage of Jacob your father,
> For the mouth of the Lord has spoken."

Sabbath rest is important for the human soul, body, mind and spirit. It's blessed me beyond words and if you have not been observing the Sabbath, I encourage you to start because keeping this special time with God is worth it!

~*~

Reflection Questions:
1. When was the last time you decided to set work aside and rest?
2. How does resting make you feel and affect your life?

Week 28

God's Protection

> If you say, "The Lord is my refuge,"
> and you make the Most High your dwelling,
> no harm will overtake you,
> no disaster will come near your tent.
> For he will command his angels concerning you
> to guard you in all your ways;
> they will lift you up in their hands,
> so that you will not strike your foot against a stone."
>
> – Psalm 91:9-12 (NIV)

One afternoon, Psalm 91:11 entered my thoughts as I observed what is becoming a familiar sight at one of my favorite town centers. As I drove into the town center, I noticed a squad of men and women dressed like secret service agents (people with "serious" no-nonsense looks on their faces who are dressed in Black slacks, Black blazers, white shirts, shiny black shoes and ear pieces to communicate with each other).

Just like the first time I saw them, they descended on the town center and set themselves up on the four corners surrounding the area in which a cupcake shop is central. They had the entire area covered. Each guarded a checkpoint. Each person looked serious as they surveyed their surroundings and if they had a weapon, it was concealed.

I do not know who these secret service agents were guarding but I think the person may be a high-profile politician or government employee given the area that the town center is located. It's only a few miles away from important places where people in power gather for business and work-related matters.

It's not the first time I've witnessed this scenario. But that was the first time that my mind drew a parallel and life lesson from this situation. I realized that just like those secret service agents guarded every corner of the area where their Very Important Person (VIP) was visiting, staying vigilant and ready to defend the VIP if needed, God sends His Angels from Heaven to guard us every single day, in every way!

The Bible says in, Psalm 91:11, "For He will give His angels charge concerning you, to guard you in all your ways."

There's a song by Virtue called "Angels Watching Over Me" that speaks to God's protection for humankind. The lyrics tell the listener that God's Angels surround humans, protecting them from harm. But they do more than protect; they remind you (maybe not audibly, but by an impression on your heart or a word in your spirit) that God loves you! They cover you with God's grace and they want to see you make it to Heaven. God's Angels watch over you 24/7/365. They never need a lunch break or time to sleep.

It's comforting to know that God's Angels are always watching over you and me, guarding us and delivering us from evil. They are stronger and smarter than the world's best-trained secret service agents and unlike mere mortals like you and me, they will never fail an assignment to cover us. They cannot be killed, and they are very skilled at doing God's will.

The Bible also says in Psalm 34:7, "The angel of the Lord encamps around those who fear Him, and He delivers them."

Situations in life can be scary but you don't have to be a VIP to be covered by God's protection. God has promised to be with you wherever you go. He will *never* leave you or forsake you. He's holding you close in His Hand and taking care of you from the moment He wakes you up in the morning (believe it or not, it's not our alarm clock that wakes us up) to the moment you go to sleep for the night then His angels are on guard as you sleep!

God's protection over all of His children here on Earth is a 24/7/365 operation. He has unlimited resources to help us and deliver us from evil. If you believe in God, you've already got a protection squad in the form of His Heavenly Angels. You may not be able to see them but they are always with you. God's Angels are here to help us make it through our journey here on Earth. Hebrews 1:4 (KJV) says, "Are they not all ministering spirits, sent forth to minister for them who shall be heirs of salvation?"

Next time you're in a situation that scares you, ask God to send His protection. Pray for His protection even when you cannot sense danger or think that everything is okay. Remember, God sees what we cannot see and He protects us more than we may think! So don't only ask God for protection, *thank* Him for it!

Trust and believe that your Creator (God) loves you. He is there for you, sending His Angels to protect you and guard you in all your ways. Best of all, you don't need an earpiece to communicate with God, He's only prayer away *and* He knows what you need even before you pray!

Perhaps God's Protection can be summed up in the words of Isaiah 65:24 (KJV) in which He says, "And it shall come to pass, that before they call, I will answer; and while they are yet speaking, I will hear."

Isn't God Awesome?

~*~

Reflection Questions:
1. How does it feel to know that God's Angels are always protecting you?
2. Did you know that you are God's VIP (very important person)?

Week 29

The Christian Life

"It's not the devil's plan to *convert* us but to simply *divert* us."

– Pastor Peter Bath

Pastor Peter Bath is one wise preacher because in that simple quote, he uncovered a key strategy of the enemy—the devil sends diversions that rob us of our joy, peace and patience. If we're not careful, the devil's ploys can also rob us of our salvation which is why the Holy Bible tells us to put on the "full armor of God" every day (Ephesians 6:11-18) for the battles we are facing are not with "flesh and blood" but with against principalities, powers and "spiritual wickedness in high places."

Did you think that the person who cut you off on the freeway was your enemy or the person who offended you was your true problem? What about the new barista working in your favorite café who gets the order for your favorite cup of coffee wrong and since you're already running late to work, you cannot wait for the barista to correct your order? What about the boss who doesn't seem to like you or the colleague who has it in for you?

No! All of these people are merely *distractions* because the *real* problem is *not* with the person who cut you off on the freeway or the person you don't like because they offended you. There is a deeper level to life happening every day and Christians are on the frontlines.

> "The Christian life is not a playground. It's a battleground."
>
> – Pastor Steven Furtick

Pastor Furtick is another man of God who is wise and on-point with his sermons. His creative team at Elevation Church based in North Carolina, created a video message, "I Will Fight" that is very inspirational and true to what I'm telling you today. If you need encouragement in your journey, watch the video.

Here are a few quotes from Pastor Furtick's motivational message, "I Will Fight":

"The devil is a liar and my God always causes me to triumph through Jesus Christ my Lord. I will fight. I'm unashamed to represent a kingdom that is unshakable. No one will be able to stand against God's plan for me all the days of my life. With my God, I will advance against every troop, with His help, I will scale every wall. Though my enemies surround me, my God surrounds my enemies. Though they may come at me one way, they will flee seven ways because no weapon formed against me will prosper and every evil thing that rises against me, I will condemn. I will fight! My heart is steadfast, my purpose is immovable. I am always abounding in the work of the Lord and my potential is unlimited because the limitless God lives within me. I will fight!"

Now that's an attitude we *all* need to have as Christians. Don't let the enemy discourage or divert you. It's his plan to divert your focus from God and emphasize the troubles and despair of this world. But there is *hope* because God is *more powerful* than the enemy and clearly the Bible tells us in the Book of Revelation that at the end of human history, God wins!

Stay on the winning side by keeping your faith in God alive and strong. Don't be overwhelmed by the magnitude of the battles you face in this life. Remember, you can be victorious in this life through Jesus Christ! The Bible says, "If God is for us, who can be against us?" (Romans 8:31)

So take heart as you remember these simple truths: God loves you (John 3:16). God is for you (Romans 8:31). God will never leave you nor forsake you (Hebrews 13:5) and you can have the victory in Jesus Christ our Lord and Savior (1 Corinthians 15:57)!

I think we've reached the point in this devotional where if we were in church service, the pastor would say, "And let the church say Amen."

~*~

Reflection Questions:
1. How has your faith in God encouraged you to fight when times are tough?
2. In what ways has keeping your faith in God strong helped you to survive?

Week 30

What's Your Motivation?

"I have been crucified with Christ; it is no longer I who live, but Christ lives in me; and the *life* which I now live in the flesh I live by faith in the Son of God, who loved me and gave Himself for me."

– Galatians 2:20 (NKJV)

When actors are working on a movie, they always ask the director, "What's my character's motivation?" or "What does my character want in this scene?"

Allow me to clarify and explain: The actor is not asking for their motivation as an actor, they're asking for the motivation of the character that they are portraying. The actor needs to know their fictional character's motivation in order to properly act it out. Their motivation determines how the character would act. Therefore, when an actor knows this information, it determines how the actor will portray the character.

Actress Jenn Gotzon Chandler said, "Motivation is why a character does something. Why a character makes choices, why a character feels certain ways about other people.

As a Christian fiction writer, I've learned the importance of determining the emotional, physical and spiritual goal/motivation/conflict (GMC) of my fictional characters *before* starting the story because for me as a writer, knowing these details helps me to not only deeply understand my characters but it determines how I write the story.

When I know my character's motivation in their fictional life then I know why they have certain goals and I know what kind of conflict is needed to make their journey interesting and worthwhile. Knowing my characters' GMC makes the story. It helps me to guide their every step because I know what they are moving toward, and as the creator of the story, I know the best route for them to take in order reach their destination in "the end."

Recently, I was thinking about this and I realized there is a parallel to real life in all of this because God is our Creator, this world is His creation, and He is the Director of this movie called Life. Famous our not, we *all* have a part to play in this movie and nobody can portray our character better than we can because God created us to be unique.

As our Divine Director, God already knows our deepest desires and He is well aware of our motivation. But unlike most movies, we as the characters in the movie of Life are able to determine our destiny because God gave us free will. So the choice is ours. It's up to us to determine our motivation.

There's a song by Plumb called "Lord I'm Ready Now." Let's look at my paraphrase of the song lyrics. The singer starts off at the point of letting God know that she's finally let go and given Him control. But this decision has left her feeling exposed yet she realizes that this kind of exposure is a beautiful thing because she is showing her true self and not hiding how God made her. She acknowledges that she's made a mess out of her life but she also doesn't care because she realizes that time to live on Earth will run out and she wants to focus on what's eternal. She wants to live for God and make it to Heaven. Her new motivation to live for Him changes everything in her life for the better. She's grateful for the second chance that God's given her and she's sold out for Jesus.

Plumb says the story behind her song comes from a point in her life when her husband left her and she became a single mother of three children. She went through a dark time and couldn't see the light. But she stood on the promises of God found in His Word (The Holy Bible) and fell in love with Jesus Christ for the very first time. Finally, she realized that fame and fortune do not last but what you do for Jesus Christ such as making a difference in someone's life is the only thing that lasts for all eternity.

When she gave her life to Jesus and let Him take the pen in writing her story, starting over with God in mind, that's when God restored all she had lost and gave her a new perspective and outlook on life. Now she has a whole new approach to her music, it's more of a ministry now, not a vehicle to fame and fortune. Following Jesus Christ and living for God is Plumb's motivation.

In closing, I'd like to inform you that *you* are a star in this movie called Life. You have the choice every day to live for Jesus and allow Him to transform your life in ways that will have an eternal impact. Will you accept this role of following Him?

~*~

Reflection Questions:
1. As a star in the movie of Life, what's your motivation?
2. What is it about Plumb's story that touches your heart?

Week 31

A Happily Ever After that Never Ends

> "And God shall wipe away all tears from their eyes; and there shall be no more death, neither sorrow, nor crying, neither shall there be any more pain: for the former things are passed away."
>
> – Revelation 21:4 (KJV)

This devotional is based on the end quote in a movie that I saw a year ago on The Hallmark Channel, "Love By The Book."

"Love By The Book" is a movie about a hopeless romantic who grew up with as steady serving of fairy tales. So at a very young age, she fully embraced the storybook concept of meeting Prince Charming, marrying him and living happily ever after. Now as an adult, that's what she's looking for in the dating scene. But after kissing many "frogs" she's failed at the perfect book romance that her heart so desires and starts to question her fairy tale beliefs.

I watched this movie almost two years ago, so I do not recall the intricacies of the plot. But I do recall quite clearly the end quote from the hero to the heroine at the end of the movie. He told the heroine, "Do you know what I don't like about happily ever afters? After happily ever after, the story ends."

Such a line made faith and fiction collide in my mind! Allow me to spend the next few paragraphs explaining what I realized in that moment.

As believers in God and followers of Jesus Christ, we have a promise that our life story will not end permanently after we reach "the end" of our life. We can rest in the truth that if we lived for Jesus Christ and followed Him during our lives here on Earth then when He returns, He will take us home to heaven. There, in that perfect place, we will experience an unparalleled happily ever after that rivals Cinderella and every other perfect fairy tale book ending and it's unrivaled because this happily ever after never ends!

There are verses in the Bible that talk about how we'll "walk the streets of gold" (Revelation 21:21) in Heaven. God, who created you, will wipe away all of the tears that were caused by your deep pain and devastation that you faced while living on Earth.

Let's read Revelation 21:4 (KJV). It says, "And God shall wipe away all tears from their eyes; and there shall be no more death, neither sorrow, nor crying, neither shall there be any more pain: for the former things are passed away."

Never again will you have to kiss a loved one goodbye as cancer or another disease claims their life. There will be no need for insurance of any type because everything will be perfect and death will not happen to anyone or anything ever again. You'll get to talk with God and Jesus Christ in person and live forever in a perfect body!

I don't know about you, but such a wonderful promise of eternal life in a sin-free existence makes my heart happy! Who needs a fictional fairy tale "happily ever after" that ends the story forever, when you have a real-life promise that if you believe in Jesus and follow Him then you *will* live happily ever after with the Prince of Peace (Jesus Christ), for *eternity*?

There's a beautiful song by Kari Jobe called "Forever." The song lyrics showcase who God is and what His Son Jesus Christ endured so that we may have a second chance at salvation. The lyrics describe how God's creation (earth, moon, stars, everything) grieved Christ's death on the cross. It is because of His death that the price of our sins was paid and it is because of His resurrection three days later, that we have hope because He is Alive and He's interceding on our behalf before our Heavenly Father. So when God sees us (sinners), He remembers that the blood of His Son (Jesus) covers our sins so that He can forgive us if we repent of our sins and ask Him.

Thanks for Christ's sacrifice, we each have the chance for the best happily ever after that the most creative fiction writers could never begin to create! We have the chance to accept Jesus into our hearts, live for Him and follow Him all the way to Heaven! This "happily ever after" ending to our human story that God is offering is one that once started, never ends! Perfection doesn't even begin to describe the beauty and peace that awaits us and no words can capture how wonderful it will feel to spend eternity in the presence of our Eternal King.

Now let's bring this message back to earth and relate it our modern day. As humans, many of us are fascinated by the Royals from around the world, but who needs to pursue earthly royalty for a happily ever after here on Earth when the Bible says that we as children of God are "joint-heirs with Christ" (Romans 8:17)? Do you know what that means? It means that *you* and *I* are adopted into God's family, which makes us royalty!

So, ladies always remember that you are a princess and gentlemen, always keep in mind that you are a prince. And always, ladies *and* gentlemen, remember that your Heavenly Father is King of kings, Lord of lords, the Creator of the Universe and is waiting to bless you with a happily ever after that lasts for all of eternity.

~*~

Reflection Questions:
1. How does it feel to know that a Happily Ever After (HEA) does exist not only in fiction stories, but in real life for all those who follow Jesus Christ?
2. How does it feel to know that when you accept Jesus into your heart, you become a child of the Eternal King (God) and that makes you royalty?

Week 32

Enduring Love

> "Give thanks to the God of heaven. *His faithful love endures forever.*"
>
> – Psalm 136:26 (NLT)

When we hear those sacred and treasured words "I love you too" from someone who we love – romantically or platonically – after we've said, "I love you," it can put us on a high.

Why? Because someone we love revealed that they love us too! There is nothing like love that is reciprocated.

Whenever someone who I love tells me that they love me too, their words warm my heart and I feel like I can live off of those kind words for days.

But lately, I have been thinking that mankind is not meant to live off of words spoken by people they love; we are supposed to live off of God's Words that are found in The Holy Bible, also known as God's Love Letter to humankind.

Why is it so important to live off the Word of God? Because God's Words give life! There is a reason why the Bible says, "Man shall not live on bread alone, but on every word that comes from the mouth of God." (Matthew 4:4)

His Word – not the love, praise or compliments of humankind – sustains us and prepares us for eternity spent with Him in Heaven. His Word – not our paychecks, sports car, full bank account, dream house, spouse or anything else here on Earth – makes life worth living! God's Word has the capacity to change us from the inside-out, encourage our heart, strengthen our soul, bless our mind and lead people to Him!

Life isn't about gaining and maintaining the love of your fellow humans; it's about entering into a relationship with the Savior of the world (Jesus Christ) and following Him all the way to Heaven. The God of Heaven who is the Creator of humankind and King of the Universe, loves *you* with *all* of His Heart! He sent His Son (Jesus Christ) to Earth in order to save your soul (John 3:16). All you have to do is accept Him as your Savior and believe in Him then as I said earlier, follow Him all the way to Heaven.

And as for love, God's love for *you* endures forever! You are the apple of His eye (Zechariah 2:8), the treasure of His Heart (Deuteronomy 7:6). He cannot imagine life without you, which is why He sent His Son to save you!

God promises to be with you forever (Matthew 28:20). His love for you will not fail (Psalm 136:1). You are His child (Galatians 3:26) and He is a Good Father (Matthew 7:11).

Let's take a moment to really wrap our minds around this: The Creator of the *Universe* loves *you* and His Love for *you* endures forever!

Knowing that my Maker loves me with all of His Heart and knowing that He'll never leave more nor forsake me (Hebrews 13:5), gives me peace!

Knowing that God loves me and has good plans for my life (Jeremiah 29:11) makes my heart happy!

Knowing that the Savior of this world wants to be my Best Friend and wants to see me through trials on this Earth and bless me with eternal life as I follow Him all the way to Heaven, astounds me as I realize that there is no other love is like His!

Knowing that there's nothing I can do to make God love me less or to make Him love me more because He loves me (and you) unconditionally, gives my mind a peace that passes all understanding (Philippians 4:7) and fills me with the kind of hope that this world cannot offer.

Knowing that God's love for me (and you) endures forever is such a beautiful truth. Knowing that I love Him and He loves me is the best kind of reciprocated love out there!

As I close this devotional, I'd like for you to listen to Jaci Velasquez sing the song "God Loves You" ... it's like a hug for your heart!

Listen to the song and be soothed as Jaci reminds you of God's heart for you. Be encouraged as she assures you that He is always there for you so you are never truly alone. I love how she says in her song that God will love you, comfort you and set you free! Remember that He is the light in the darkness. You've got the most powerful force in the universe watching out for you!

God loves you, dear friend. Do you love Him?

Reflection Questions:
1. Recall the first time that you felt God's love for you. What life lesson did it teach you?
2. What Bible verse can you cling to when you need a reminder of God's love for you?

Week 33

A Different Kind of Overwhelmed

"Have you ever felt overwhelmed and all-consumed with love for someone? Maybe a spouse or a child? God wants you to be overwhelmed with His love for you."

– Pastor Rick of K-LOVE

The Merriam-Webster Dictionary definition for the word "overwhelmed" that we're going to focus on for this devotional is that it means to "to cover over completely."

Have you ever felt covered over completely by life's problems, trials and tribulations? Have you ever felt like you were sinking deep into a metaphorical ocean and almost drowning beneath the weight of it all?

If you answered, "Yes" to either of those questions then today's devotional is for you!

I want to put a positive spin on the definition of overwhelmed today. I want to teach you about a different kind of "overwhelmed": The kind where you are *covered completely* by God's Love.

Lately, I've been feeling overwhelmed by the worries of this world and personal issues in my own life. However, after visiting K-LOVE radio station's official website and reading this blog post called "Experiencing God's Love" that was written by K-LOVE Pastor Rick, I realized that God wants me to experience a different kind of overwhelmed—the kind where I feel completely covered by His love for me! This truth put everything in perspective for me.

Why?

Because I realized that when I take time to meditate on God's Word (The Holy Bible), it causes me to remember how much He loves me which then causes my problems and the worries of this world start to slowly but surely fade away. As the worries fade, God's Goodness, Grace, Love, Mercy and Majesty flood in, making me acutely aware of who He is (Lord over *all*, according to Psalm 97:9) and showing me that He wants to help me survive the trials of life. When this happens, no longer do I worry about the troubles of today or have anxiety about tomorrow because I know that God is in control.

It's in those moments that God's Love overwhelms me. It's a beautiful place to be, wrapped in the center of love from the heart of the Sovereign King who created me, you, our planet Earth, and the entire *universe*!

When you spend time meditating on God's Word (The Holy Bible) and applying His Truth to your everyday life, it's hard to *not* feel the sheer magnitude of how good God is and it's hard to *not* experience the steadfast, fierce, grace-filled, *forever love* that He has for you!

And when you're in those moments, completely basking in God's love, you realize that this is a different kind of overwhelmed...a very good one that produces peace that passes all understanding (Philippians 4:7) and gives you hope for tomorrow.

STORIES AND SONGS OF FAITH

There is joy found in God's presence! There is peace, hope and happiness!

God won't force you to experience His Love because He gives us all the free will to choose Him or deny Him. The Bible says in Revelation 3:20 that He stands at the door and knocks, waiting for us to invite Him in. However, He is patient with us because He wants us *all* to be experience His Love and be saved in His Kingdom that is not of this world.

When you allow yourself to experience the overwhelming love of God, it transforms you from the inside out! After that experience, it's almost impossible for you to *not* love others after you see how much God loves you! His Love for you creates hope in your heart that whatever you're worried about will be resolved in His perfect time and it also creates deep empathy for everyone else created by God.

Part of experiencing this "different kind of overwhelmed" is not being able to put your experience with God into words. I think I tried my best in this devotional but in closing, I'd like to share a song by Jasmine Murray that really drives my point home. The song is called "Into Words."

It is impossible for me put God "into words" because He is beyond words! His goodness is forever, just like His love for humankind withstands the test of time. He loves you with *all* of His Heart and wants you to choose Him.

It's overwhelming but in a very *good* way!

~*~

Reflection Questions:
1. How does leaning into God when you're feeling overwhelmed help you?
2. How does knowing that you are completely covered by God's love comfort you?

Week 34

Our Forever Friend

"One who has unreliable friends soon comes to ruin, but there is a friend who sticks closer than a brother."

– Proverbs 18:24 (NIV)

Recently, I re-read a mini-devotional thought that is located within a sidebar on the pages of my *True Identity* Bible, published by Zondervan.

The title of the mini-devotional thought was "At Issue: Loneliness."

Here is what I read:

"In the beloved book *Anne of Green Gables*, Anne longs for a "bosom friend." Can you relate? Unfortunately, most of us have known the pain at times of not having a close friend. Yet loneliness is not entirely bad. Painful as it is, loneliness is good when it pushes us to grow closer to the best friend we'll ever have—God. No other friendship can compare to his. He knows and accepts us completely. He is right there with us, always. In the good times we take our friend for granted. In the bad times we realize we need him – and he's right there."

Though I've read the devotional countless times before, this time that I re-read it really struck a chord with me. Finally, it dawned on me that I already have the best kind of friend anyone can have, his name is Jesus Christ and He loves humankind with His life! Read John 3:16-17 in The Holy Bible.

Yes, I know the pain of feeling left out. Not always having a best friend here on Earth. Not having the "Maid of Honor" experience in my best friend's wedding. Not being a bridesmaid several times over in all of my close friends' weddings. Not having as Anne of Green Gables called it, a "bosom friend."

But, I do also know the unexplainable JOY that comes when Jesus Christ is your best friend for life! Literally. His friendship will never fade. He will be your best friend here on Earth and in Heaven, forever (literally again)!

And that truth brings me hope. It also gives me a fresh perspective. Because it can be so easy for us – especially females – because of the culture that we live in, to feel left out if our social lives don't look like what we see on TV, at the movies and on social media.

But just because you see those worldly standards for friendships all around you, you don't have to believe that those representations of life are how your life should look. You don't have to subscribe to worldly standards of living.

Yes, it's great to be included. Yes, it's great to have a best friend or a circle of close friends. Yes, it's wonderful if God blessed you with one special bosom friend like Anne of Green Gables had in Diana.

But if you do *not* have that yet then don't worry about it; pray about it!

Trust God to bring the people into your life who need to be there. And if He blesses you with a "bosom friend" or a close-knit, healthy circle of friends then praise Him! But don't forget to cultivate your relationship with the *one friend who will never leave you nor forsake you* (Hebrews 13:5) ... that friend is Jesus Christ!

I hope that this devotional has encouraged your heart.

In closing, I'd like for you to listen to this song, "Forever Yours," by Wintley Phipps.

Allow me to paraphrase the song: He starts off by painting a beautiful picture of a quiet place where he feels close enough to God to see God's face. As he spends time with God, he can hear God's voice speak to his soul. This closeness to God fills him with love and gratitude to the point where he makes a vow to God telling Him that he is "Forever Yours." He then realizes that he needs to keep his commitment to spend time with God faithfully. He feels saddened by the times he strayed from God's side and reassures God that he will be His forever. He wants to give his life to God and live for Him forever. It is clear through the song lyrics that this singer (Wintley Phipps) loves God.

The song is a pledge of devotion from one of God's children to God's heart. It's beautiful. But it doesn't have to only be a song performed by a famous musician; this devotion can be your reality! God wants all of His children to be devoted to Him and when you enter into a saving relationship with His Son Jesus Christ (if you haven't already), your heart will be moved to want to belong to God forever and you'll see why He's the most wonderful Heavenly Father, Creator and Friend.

Jesus truly is the truest friend that anyone could have in this life on Earth and in Heaven. He is fully invested in you. He cares about every detail of your life and only He can save your soul! If you're lonely, cry out to Jesus! He will stay by your side. God truly is the best kind of forever friend.

~*~

Reflection Questions:
1. Have you longed for a best friend?
2. How does it feel to know that the Creator of the Universe wants to be your friend forever?

Week 35

God's Not Going Anywhere

"And surely I am with you always, to the very end of the age."
– Matthew 28:20b (NIV)

God taught me a lesson one day when I was worried that I might be losing a close friend who I hadn't heard from in a while. I remember thinking to myself that all I need to hear from that friend was, "I love you" and "Don't worry. I'm not going anywhere."

For me, that would reassure me that though they've been silent for a while, they still care about me and I'm not losing my connection or friendship with that person. As this has been on my mind a lot, God impressed me with a spiritual lesson related to it. He spoke to my heart saying, "But Alexis. I love you and I am not going anywhere!"

God reminded me that even if people let me down, He wouldn't. God taught me years ago that though He may be silent at times, He's not going anywhere, meaning He's promised to be there for me throughout the ceaseless ages of eternity.

When God imparted this lesson to me in my spirit one night when I was wide-awake with worry about losing friends, His words encouraged my soul.

He also reminded me that His connection with me is the only connection that I should always keep alive and never worry about losing because He loves me and *all* of His children around the world, way too much to ever let us go.

God is in a relationship with us for the long haul.

He knows us better than our closest friend or even our Mamas. He sees our flaws. He hears our heart and He loves us no matter what! We can trust Him with *everything*, including our very life! His love for us will *never fail*.

Only God is completely capable of being there for us at any time and in any situation. We can rely on Him better than we could ever depend on any human. God wants us to seek Him first, not earthly friends. Now earthly friends are important to have and we should cultivate healthy relationships with people but at the same time, we should never lose sight of staying connected to the truest Best Friend we could ever have (God).

And if a friendship here on Earth is keeping us from bettering our relationship with God or moving us to lose sight of Jesus Christ, our Savior, then we should pray about it and if God tells us to let it go, we should obey.

The best thing about being friends with God is that not only does He always have our best interest at heart, there's nothing we can do to make Him love us less or love us more. He loves us because He created us. We are His.

God's love for you and me is fierce and forever! The Bible says that He will be with us until the "end of the age" (Matthew 28:20 NIV). This proves that God will be with us until the very end of human history (also known as the end of the world). But for those of us who believe in Him, our life story doesn't stop there.

God will usher His faithful followers into an eternity spent with Him where we will live in healthy, immortal bodies forever!

Finally there will be no more death, sorrow, pain, destruction or natural disasters; there will only be joy, freedom, happiness and hope that will last forever! We will grow into all God originally intended us to be! We will live completely free of sin and all of the mass destruction it causes. But meanwhile, as we journey through this Earth and go through the various seasons of life that include joy and sorrow, it gives me hope to know that God is with us and He'll never leave our side.

There's a beautiful song by CeCe Winans called "He's Always There." In the song lyrics, she shares the Bible-based truth that God is always there for you, ready to bring a smile to your face, encourage you and guide you through the seasons of life. She reminds the listener that God is patient with you when you as if your faith is faltering. He understands that you're human and sometimes frail. He encourages you ask for what you need. He wants you to believe in Him and allow Him to transform your life for the better. God promises to comfort you and love you forever.

CeCe's song encourages me because it reminds me that God will never leave me nor forsake me. He loves me (and you) and He's not going anywhere! Knowing that God is a friend who will never leave gives me comfort because I know that even if my human friendships fail, I have a Friend in Jesus and His friendship with me (and you) is forever!

~*~

Reflection Questions:
1. How does it feel to know that God will never leave you?
2. What earthly friendship has God blessed you with that reminds you of His love for you?

Week 36

God's Nudge

> "And it shall come to pass, that before they call, I will answer; and while they are yet speaking, I will hear."
>
> – Isaiah 65:24 (KJV)

There have been times when God "nudged" me to do something for someone or say something to someone and I admit that I have not always listened. But one Saturday evening, I'm so glad that listened to Him and followed through with what He wanted me to do because it blessed the heart of a dear friend of mine.

On that Saturday evening, I felt nudged to write a text message and send it to my dear friend Temeka. But I pushed back because the words that were on my heart to say were what she already knew.

I know that she's strong in her convictions and not easily swayed by the ways of the world. I didn't want to "preach to the choir" so I debated with God (silently) with thoughts along the lines of...*Lord, she knows this already! She's one of the strongest women I know. She serves you wholeheartedly. She doesn't give into peer pressure. Seriously? You want me to write this? I don't want to preach to the choir. Lord, are You sure that You want me to share this with her or keep it to myself? Is this really a nudge from You, or is this just a thought from my own mind?*

After two (maybe four) full hours of off and on debate with God, I gave in and decided to send the text message and I am so glad that I did!

Temeka replied to my text immediately, saying that my message was on time and that it confirmed something that she recently talked to God about. She ended her text to me saying, "God used you!"

Wow, I thought. *God used me.*

But the praise report of how God used me to help Temeka didn't end there. She felt compelled to share her story on social media a few times—once on her personal Facebook page and again in one of her motivational videos the following week! She was overwhelmed with gratitude and I am grateful that I obeyed God's nudge and sent the message to her when He asked me to.

I don't want to imagine what would have happened if I hadn't obeyed God. Though I do know that He has many ways of helping His children here on Earth so the message would have reached Temeka somehow and still been on time. But it humbles me and strikes me with deep awe to know that God felt the need to use me to help someone who I care about and respect.

There's a song performed by the Maranatha Singers called "He Knows My Name" that speaks to the fact that God knows you better than anyone and He's always there for you. The lyrics essentially talk about God as your maker who formed your heart, which means He knows your deepest desire. God holds your life in His hands. He knows what you are thinking without your saying a word. He sees you when you cry and He answers you when you call – the

Bible says even *before* you call (Isaiah 65:24). Your life is safe in His hands. God is your Heavenly Father. You are His. He will always be there for you through thick and thin. He truly is your Best Friend. And He wants to use you to help His children see Him. Sometimes, God may use you just by causing you to give a warm smile to somebody that will brighten their day, or He may ask you to bless somebody financially. There are many ways in which God may nudge you to help someone.

Though God nudged me to help my friend Temeka by sending encouraging words that spoke to her situation, I do realize God doesn't need me to accomplish His will. Nothing is impossible with God. But it's always an honor when the Creator of the Universe asks us to do something for Him!

Next time when you feel a nudge from God, will you allow Him to use you?

~*~

Reflection Questions:
1. When was the first time that you felt a nudge from God?
2. How has obeying God's nudge in the past helped you?

Week 37

Before I Call

> "Before they call I will answer; while they are still speaking I will hear."
> – Isaiah 65:24 (NIV)

One day, God answered a prayer that I did not pray. His providence amazes me! Allow me to tell you the story of the time when God answered me before I called.

It was an ordinary weekend. The food supply in the house was low, but I didn't have money to buy groceries. I found myself thinking, *I wish I had money to go to Panera, but I need to save my money to pay bills.* So I determined to do without. I stayed home and went about my business.

A few hours later, I was talking to a writer friend who I was helping by providing feedback on certain elements in her story. She told me that she appreciated my time and talent, so she wanted to give me a gift as a thank you for my pro bono services. She asked me to choose what I wanted and suggested options like gift cards from Amazon and Starbucks. My first thought was about my wish list of books on Amazon, so I asked for an Amazon.com gift card. So she sent that to me via e-mail within the hour.

But since our arrangement was ongoing, she'd offered to send more than one gift throughout the editorial process. And I decided, since I was craving Panera, that's what I'd ask for. But I wondered, *how?* I didn't know if Panera had e-cards. So I called a local restaurant, and they directed me to their company website where indeed there was an option to send e-gift cards. I copied the direct link and sent it to my writer friend who then agreed that my payments going forward would be e-gift cards to Panera!

After our conversation, I realized God had answered me before I called. I never stopped and prayed to Him to make a way for me to have enough extra money to go to Panera, I simply thought it and pushed the thought aside when I realized it wasn't happening right now. But God heard my thoughts, and He decided to bless me unexpectedly!

Just like God provided for me by answering my prayer before I asked, He wants to provide for you too. The Bible says that He takes care of the sparrows in the sky, and we (His children) are worth far more than sparrows, so He will definitely take care of us. My story of how God provided for me is just a small picture of the grand scheme of things that God does for His children.

God is always at work in our lives. Even when we cannot see Him or feel His presence, He's still there. The Bible says in Hebrews 13:5 that God will *never* leave or forsake us. It's a promise from His heart to ours, and God faithfully keeps *all* of His promises!

I'm still growing in my faith walk with God, and I love it when He reminds me of Bible verses that apply to my experience. The Bible verse that speaks to my recent experience involving my desire for Panera reminds me of Isaiah 65:24 (NIV) in which God says, "Before they call I will answer; while they are still speaking I will hear."

It delights my soul that God taught me a lesson of His providence through answering my unspoken prayer regarding my desire for food from Panera. He used this to remind me that He cares about every detail as big as paying a mortgage to as small as buying a favorite meal from your favorite café.

I'd like to encourage you to go to God first with your every concern, request, and praise report. Then trust Him to provide for your every need… and sometimes your wants too! Trust that sometimes, even before you go to Him in prayer, He'll hear you and answer your heart's desire in a totally unexpected way like He did for me. Why? Because before we call, God will answer; while we are yet speaking, God will hear!

In closing, I'd like to share this song by Wayne Watson called "When God's People Pray." It's very encouraging. The lyrics essentially say that when you face stormy days and tough seasons in life, God is faithful. He is just a prayer away. You can call on Him and He will not only be near you; He will help you! God encourages us to take our pain to His throne in Heaven (through prayer). Only God can infuse hope into what looks like a hopeless situation and only He can turn a life around. With God in your life, you will always have hope and when you pray, He can make miracles that people cannot explain. They won't know how it happened but you will because you God did that miracle for you! Sometimes the miracles are big but in my case with the desire for Panera, the miracle was very small but so satisfying! Be encouraged to talk to God through prayer. Tell Him what's on your heart. He's always listening and ready to work a miracle for you.

~*~

Reflection Questions:
1. What do you need to talk to God about through prayer?
2. When was the last time God answered your prayers?

Week 38

On the Clock God

"My help comes from the Lord, the Maker of heaven and earth."

– Psalm 121:2 (NIV)

This devotional was inspired by a scene from my real-life work as a seasonal sales associate. One day, I went to ask our on-duty manager a question and he stepped back with his hands raised in mid-air saying kindly "I'm off the clock." Seconds later, the new manager on duty who was standing in his place while he was on break, stepped forward to address my concern.

This interaction, though very brief, taught me an important lesson. Apart from being more mindful about when a manager is off the clock, it taught me to remember that God is always *on* the clock and it gave me hope that we serve an "on the clock God."

Sometimes, when looking for the perfect Bible verse to support a devotional that you're writing, it's necessary to share the entire chapter in the Bible because it's beautiful and provides a strong support. This was the case when I set out to write this devotional "On the Clock God" and found Psalm 121 to be the best support for my message. I think that you will be delighted to know that the Brooklyn Tabernacle Choir sings this song "My Help (Cometh from the Lord)." Their voices are beautiful, the melody is captivating, and the song lyrics are inspired by the Bible verses found in Psalm 121.

Before I delve deeper into my message, would you join me in reading this beautiful passage? I've quoted the New International Version (NIV) of this Scripture.

Psalm 121
A song of ascents.

I lift up my eyes to the mountains—
where does my help come from?
My help comes from the Lord,
the Maker of heaven and earth.
He will not let your foot slip—
he who watches over you will not slumber;
indeed, he who watches over Israel
will neither slumber nor sleep.
The Lord watches over you—
the Lord is your shade at your right hand;
the sun will not harm you by day,
nor the moon by night.
The Lord will keep you from all harm—
he will watch over your life;
the Lord will watch over your coming and going
both now and forevermore.

This beautiful passage of Scripture inspires my heart and comforts my soul. Why? Because my dear friends, it reminds me that we were created by a God who is always on the clock! He never slumbers. He's never on break. He's there for us 24/7/365 no matter what and He's readily available to come to our rescue!

I find it so incredibly comforting that God is always there for me and that He'll *never* leave or forsake me (Hebrews 13:5). It soothes my soul to know that not only is God available 24/7/365 but He's also completely capable of helping me in *every* situation! The Bible clearly says that the only thing God *cannot* do is *fail* (Joshua 21:45). He's better than our fictional heroes like Superman and Wonder Woman because He's *real*, He created us (so he knows us better than anyone here on Earth) *and* His life span is eternal (so He cannot and *will not* ever die).

So, my dear hearts, whenever you have a problem or concern in this life, don't hesitate to take it to God first. He loves you will of His divine heart and He wants to hear from you.

God wants to be your first resort for any problem you may face. He wants you to trust Him and confide in Him like you would with your dearest friend or loved one. Since He never slumbers, don't feel afraid or hesitant to call Him in your midnight hour. He will come to your rescue and help you in ways that our mere mortals cannot but that doesn't mean that He won't use His people here on Earth to help you too. God is good and He loves to bless you through His servants (followers of Jesus Christ) throughout the world!

Aren't you glad that we serve and on the clock God?

Reflection Questions:
1. How does it make you feel to know that God is never off the clock?
2. When was the last time that you went to God as your first resort?

Week 39

Shelter in the Rain

> "God is our refuge and strength, always ready to help in times of trouble."
>
> – Psalm 46:1 (NLT)

Today, I'd like to share a real-life story about a time when God provided shelter in the rain for me, literally!

Back in the days of my college years, I would have to walk several blocks off campus for an assignment. I am usually prepared for everything weather-wise but when I started walking away from the campus on that day, the sun was shining, and the weather was fair. So I did not bring my umbrella or a coat because I didn't think I'd need it.

After completing my assignment, I headed back to my campus. The first two minutes were blessed with fair weather but then the clouds rolled in, the sky grew overcast and rain started to pour. By that time, I still had two more blocks to walk before I reached the campus.

Silently, I reprimanded myself for not being prepared for the change of weather. Just as silently, I braced myself and accepted the reality that I was going to be soaked from head to toe by the time I arrived on campus. So I clutched my books close to my chest and plugged forward—not moving too fast so that I could prevent from falling on the sidewalk that was becoming slippery as the water coated it.

Clearly, I was not prepared for this unexpected downpour. But after about four minutes of walking in the rain, God sent shelter in the rain. I looked to my left as a small metro bus pulled up alongside me and stopped. The door opened and the driver beckoned me.

I stepped into the metro bus and slid into the front seat behind the driver. The door shut. I looked around and saw that I was the only passenger. He did not ask me to pay a fare. He simply started a conversation as he drove me the remaining two blocks back to my college campus.

The conversation was light and humorous. He told me that rainy days like this one make me as a student, fall in love even more with my books. He was funny. After a two-minute drive (because wheels are faster than feet walking in the rain), he stopped and opened the door. I stepped off the bus and thanked him. He waved goodbye, shut the metro bus door and drove away.

I had arrived safely on campus and only had to walk a few paces to my dorm where I promptly went to my room and changed into dry clothes.

My lesson learned (apart from always carry an umbrella and a coat)? *God is our Shelter in the Rain.*

He pulls up alongside of us and offers to carry us through tough times.

Life is better when you go through it with God. The Bible says to draw near to God and He will draw near to you (James 4:8). But just like The Parable of the Lost Sheep (Luke 15), God seeks you out even when you don't make it your will to draw near to Him. He is always present, a true gentleman who won't force His way into Your heart but will ask You to open the door to Him so that He may come in and sup with you (Revelation 3:20).

And just when we think that we're unprepared to weather the storms of life, God always makes a way—even when we don't pray—to help us survive.

I did not pray for shelter in the rain on that day, but God knew what I needed and He sent shelter in the form of that bus. I am forever grateful that God is faithful and always present for His children.

My experience on that day reminds me of the hymn "A Shelter in the Time of Storm." The refrain stands out to me the most because it paints the picture of how the raging storms may surround us yet in the middle of those torrential rains that threaten to take us under, God provides a safe place. He is our shelter.

In closing, I'd like to share this Bible verse:

> "God is our shelter and strength, always ready to help in times of trouble. So we will not be afraid, even if the earth is shaken and mountains fall into the ocean depths; even if the seas roar and rage, and the hills are shaken by the violence. There is a river that brings joy to the city of God, to the sacred house of the Most High. God is in that city, and it will never be destroyed; at early dawn he will come to its aid. Nations are terrified, kingdoms are shaken; God thunders, and the earth dissolves. The Lord Almighty is with us; the God of Jacob is our refuge."
>
> – Psalm 46:1-7 (GNT)

May you always trust God to provide your every need just like He did it for me, He can do it for you too.

~*~

Reflection Questions:
1. Think of a time when God provided exactly what you needed. How did that strengthen your faith in Him?
2. Have you ever needed shelter in the rain?

Week 40

The Rich Life

"Keep your life free from love of money, and be content with what you have, for he has said, "I will never leave you nor forsake you."

– Hebrews 13:5 (ESV)

My Dad: "Alexis, you love too much money!"

Me: "I don't *love* money; I recognize my *need* for it!"

This is a real-life script of a conversation that replays often after I vocalize my desire to be wealthy and never in need financially. Allow me to explain: For the past several years, I've been struggling financially but excelling in creative pursuits, which is part of my dream, thank God. But as with any creative person, you deal with the being a "starving artist" before you hit the big time and boy, am I still in that stage!

It can be discouraging to work so hard yet still be a "starving artist" but I've realized my need to stay grateful because I'm not "starving" in a literal sense when it comes to access to good food or agape love. I'm only starving *financially*, which is actually a blessing because I have the support of family and friends who care about me. If anything, this whole experience is teaching me to trust God with little so He can trust me with much (Luke 16:10-12). But even if He doesn't make me famous or wealthy, I will still serve Him because He is wonderful and my true treasures are in Heaven, not here on Earth.

Through it all, I'm also learning how to be content with what I have and enjoy the blessings as they are ever present. You see, I've realized that despite being financially "poor" and going through the issues related to that struggle, I am *rich* in the things that matter!

I realize that I'd rather be *rich* in the things that *do matter* than rich in the things that *don't matter*. Making a six-figure salary and being able to afford everything that my heart desires does *not* matter. But being surrounded by loved ones who support and encourage me *does* matter! Spending time with people who genuinely care about me, and not being able to afford lavish adventures is what I'd choose over gorgeous yachts, private jet planes and fancy dinners in exotic locations.

Becoming closer to God while drawing near to Him during tough times and being refreshed by His Presence and His Word is an experience that I would never trade for the world's wealth and wisdom. Why? Because everything that is part of this world, all of the material possessions that we hold dear on Earth and all of the pursuits we want to achieve, are *all fading away* as this world nears end.

So I decide to invest in eternity…an eternity spent with Jesus Christ in the places He's prepared His faithful followers in Heaven.

There's a song by Avalon called "Can't Live A Day" that really speaks to how I feel.

The song reminds the listener of what really matters in this life (it's not money). The singers say that they could survive living alone and not having their dreams come true but what they cannot do is live without God. They say that God is their heartbeat. He means more than all this world can offer. God is more wonderful than all of the wonders found in this world. No amount of riches could every compare to all that God has to offer to you. God is the source of life. The singers recognize that everything they have in this life was given to them by God. They cannot imagine facing tomorrow without Him by their side. Ultimately, they realize that they do not and cannot life a day without God. He is their Creator, Guide, Protector, Provider and most faithful Friend. They know that with God on their side, there's nothing that they cannot face victoriously.

I hope and pray that if you have not already, you will choose Jesus today! He offers the abundant life (John 10:10) and that doesn't always mean you'll be rich in money but you may be rich in time, rich in love and most importantly rich in what matters most: a true relationship with Jesus Christ.

Reflection Questions:
1. What does it mean to you to be truly rich?
2. How has knowing Jesus Christ enriched your life?

Week 41

Eternal Awards

> "Everyone who competes in the games goes into strict training. They do it to get a crown that will not last; but we do it to get a crown that will last forever."
>
> – 1 Corinthians 9:25 (NIV)

In 2019, one of my books was up for an award. It was for a major award given to Christian fiction writers, one that would advance my career and increase my chances of being represented by a literary agent. Needless to say, I was eager to find out if my book made it to the final rounds!

A few months later, I found out that my book didn't make it to the final rounds of judging, meaning that it was not selected to be a finalist which also means I had no chance of winning the award.

I was disappointed because it was, according to many other writers and readers, my "best book" yet. So I hoped that maybe the judges of this awards contest would agree. However, apparently they did not.

Most book award contests are an annual event so though I could always write a new book and enter that new book into the contest in the future, this experience has made me think about the one award that I really want to receive and the best news is, I don't have to compete for it. That award, according to 1 Corinthians 9:25, is a "crown that will last forever."

The full verse alludes to what we now call The Olympics. It talks about how the athletes who sign up to participate in these great games (held in Greece back in ancient days) first endure strict training. Modern day athletes wake up before sunrise to hit the gym, exercise and train their talent. They hire coaches and personal trainers. They give up French fries, sugar and other unhealthy foods to ensure that their body is in optimal health so that they can perform at their best, all of which increases their chances of winning the gold medal.

But 1 Corinthians 9:25 tells us essentially that all of their efforts even if they win, are in vain because their award, that gold medal or as The Bible says, "crown", will not last. Why? Because it is manmade and anything made by mankind, no matter how magnificent, will not last forever.

However, there is an award, a *real* crown that *all* people who follow Jesus Christ will receive if they keep following Him. The God-made crown is an award that will, according to 1 Corinthians 9:25, "last forever."

But it is not just a crown that awaits you if you follow Jesus, eternal life also awaits! An eternity spent with Jesus in Heaven and on the Earth made new when sin is no more and the original glories of mankind and Mother Nature are restored.

I look forward to that day, receiving that award and having a body that is healthier than an Olympic athlete. The Bible says that we will become immortal and live eternally when Jesus Christ returns to take us home to Heaven. Read 1 Corinthians 15:53-55 (NIV) for details.

It's like the song "The Best is Yet to Come," sung by Scott Krippayne.

Allow me to paraphrase the lyrics: The first words to the song show the listener that the race from Earth to Heaven is tiresome and sometimes, slow when you stumble. But God is right there by your side and He always picks you up when you fall. When you are discouraged, God gives you hope and courage to keep moving forward in life and pursuing the ultimate reward (eternal life spent in the presence of God). The song encourages the listener to remember that Heaven is real and our eternal life will start there! We are encouraged to know that we will see God face to face (in our sinful state right now, we'd die if we saw God but in Heaven, we'll be able to see Him and still live). The song reminds that listener that when you die belonging to Jesus Christ, then the best is yet to come! Heaven awaits all those of follow Jesus Christ through this life! The singer encourages us to find the joy in our trials and keep our eyes on Jesus Christ.

We need to continue following Jesus, regardless of the twists and turns of life. Don't let earthy treasures take your mind off of God. Remember that everything on Earth is temporary but God is eternal!

Earthly awards – no matter how sought after or grand – pale in comparison to the eternal award that awaits those who follow Jesus! So keep the faith and follow Jesus all the way to Heaven. The award is well worth the wait!

~*~

Reflection Questions:
1. What earthly awards have you been seeking?
2. How does it feel to know that if you follow Jesus Christ, eternal life that starts in Heaven is your award?

Week 42

Glimpses of Heaven

> "But in keeping with his promise we are looking forward to a new heaven and a new earth, where righteousness dwells."
>
> – 2 Peter 3:13 (NIV)

Sometimes in the midst of my day or night, God gives me what I call "Glimpses of Heaven."

These glimpses are enlightening moments when I realize that everything is going to be all right because our trials here on Earth are temporary and Heaven with all of its glories await!

It is in these moments that my pain seems to pale in comparison of what awaits. It is in these moments when I realize that I need to focus on what really matters – my relationship with Jesus Christ and telling the world about Him our Savior!

In these moments, God renews my mind (Romans 12:1-2) and makes me fit for His service. In these moments nothing seems as bad as it looks because I know that there is a bigger picture at hand and in the end, God wins!

These glimpses of Heaven give me hope and joy! These special moments make me feel closer to God and rejoice in His Goodness. Most importantly, these hope filled moments inspire me to take my faith walk with Jesus seriously and stay on the straight and narrow road that leads to Heaven.

I am grateful for these glimpses that usually occur when I'm spending time studying God's Word (The Holy Bible). There's something about opening that book and reading those timeless words of wisdom that revitalizes my soul.

It is in those moments of prayer and Bible study that God speaks to my spirit and lets me know that there is more to life than chasing my career dreams, being well-fed with good food, achieving total fitness in my body, meeting and marrying Mr. Right…It's just a reminder that there's so much more to this life than what we see with our human eyes. And in the end, God wins!

So that means that in this Great Controversy of good vs. evil that every human is born into, if you're on God's side then you win too! What will you win? Eternal life with Him in a place (Heaven) free of pain, sickness and sorrow…a place where everyone lives forever and death is history!

Perhaps the greatest reminder of what we as followers of Jesus Christ need to know is found in Hebrews 12:1-2 (NIV), which reads:

"Therefore, since we are surrounded by such a great cloud of witnesses, let us throw off everything that hinders and the sin that so easily entangles. And let us run with perseverance the race marked out for us, fixing our eyes on Jesus, the pioneer and perfecter of faith. For the joy set before him he endured the cross, scorning its shame, and sat down at the right hand of the throne of God."

STORIES AND SONGS OF FAITH

I am reminded of a song by Robin Mark titled, "When It's All Been Said and Done." It is a beautiful reminder about what really matters. The lyrics talk about how at the end of your life, all that matters is that you have lived for truth and devoted your life to serving God, living each day for Him. All of your accomplishments, treasures, dreams and goals will fade in comparison to the glory that awaits you in Heaven. Ultimately, only what you have done for Jesus Christ will truly matter and last. The artist (Robin Mark) praised God for His mercy and thanks Him for looking beyond human weakness and being patient with us and He transforms us into who He wants us to be. Mark reminds the listener that Heaven is your true home. Followers of Jesus Christ are just passing through this Earth.

It's an important truth to remember, especially when feeling overwhelmed by the woes and temporary trappings of this world.

When the weight of the world weighs heavily on your shoulders, turn it over to Jesus because His "yoke is easy" and His "burden is light." (Matthew 11:28-30). And when you're going through dark times, remember that there is a light at the end of that dark tunnel. Jesus Christ is the Light of the world (John 8:12) and you can trust Him to see you through!

As we close this devotional, I'd like to encourage you to ask God to give you glimpses of Heaven as you spend time with Him in Bible study and prayer. My prayer is that these glimpses will help you continue to move forward in your journey here on Earth and follow Jesus all the way to Heaven!

~*~

Reflection Questions:
1. Have you asked God to give you a glimpse of Heaven?
2. How would receiving a glimpse of Heaven encourage you in your spiritual journey?

Week 43

End of Story

> "For God so loved the world that He gave His only begotten Son, that whoever believes in Him should not perish but have everlasting life. For God did not send His Son into the world to condemn the world, but that the world through Him might be saved."
>
> – John 3:16-17 (NKJV)

Years ago, one of my college classmates, we'll call her Liz, said that whenever she picks up a new book, she always flips to the last few pages and reads that first so that she knows how the story ends. And if she does *not* like the end of the story, she will *not* read the book!

Liz's way of protecting her mind as a book reader stayed with me and I think of her words often. But I do not adopt her way of reading books because for me, to know how a story ends before I even begin doesn't bring me comfort. In fact, it throws the plot out the window and ruins my experience as a reader because I want to journey through the pages with the characters.

I want to get to know each of the featured characters and delve into their lives in their fictional story world. I like getting to know the characters. I like growing to care about what they want in life and being just as surprised as them with the plot takes a twist. Learning life lessons as their character is developed is something I enjoy. But most of all, I love it when the author gives my favorite characters a happy ending to their story! All of those highs and lows, twists and turns, challenges and victories, joy and sorrows make the story worth reading.

As Liz's way of reading books resurfaced in my mind recently, I remembered another illustration about a custodian who only had a grade level education. One day on his break from cleaning the school gym, someone saw the custodian reading The Holy Bible. The person walked up to the custodian and asked him how he could understand the Bible with only a grade level education. The custodian referred to the final book in the Bible called Revelation and replied that he did understand that "in the end, God wins!"

Now *that's* the only book of which I would read the very last chapter instead of starting at the beginning, because it comforts me to know that in the end of this story called Life that all humankind plays a role in, God wins!

God wins over pain. God wins over sorrow. God wins over death. God wins over *all* the maladies caused by sin and Satan. When the final curtain closes on human history, God wins! He reigns forever and will defeat the devil permanently. Evil will not last forever. Goodness, joy, grace, mercy, eternal life and pure love all of which are from God will prevail!

We will have a happy end to our story if we only believe in God and accept His Son Jesus Christ into our hearts! The Bible says in Acts 16:31 (ESV), "Believe in the Lord Jesus, and you will be saved, you and your household."

This beautiful hope of a happily ever after that lasts throughout the ceaseless ages of eternity reminds me of the gospel music song "Heaven's Door" by Dwight Anderson.

In the song, he describes the streets of Heaven, which are made from pure gold (Revelation 21:21). He speaks of resting upon a shore of crystal, sitting beside mighty lions unafraid and feeling the perfect peace of knowing that all of the pain and trials that he experienced while living as a citizen of Heaven (Philippians 3:20) on Earth are over!

The artist (Dwight Anderson) talks about what he wants to do when he arrives in Heaven. He wants to see the Mercy Seat (Exodus 25:17-22), meet his guardian angel, walk with famous Bible characters like Moses and Elijah, talk with Jesus forever and use the wings of his new, immortal body to soar to all of the other worlds that God created!

But this is more than a dream for Dwight, this is going to be the beautiful reality for all who accept Jesus Christ and believe in God!

Heaven is *real*, my friends. God is *real* and salvation offered through God's Son (Jesus Christ) is the *real* deal that leads to eternal life spent in the presence of God the Father forever!

So won't you join me on this journey to Heaven? Won't you pick up a copy of the book about the Greatest Story ever told (The Holy Bible), open it and get to know the Savior of the World (Jesus Christ) as you read His Word?

Start in the book of Genesis (where the story begins) then turn each page, experiencing the highs and lows with the characters, knowing that by the time you reach the end of your journey through God's Word (reading the last chapter in the book of Revelation), that the end of the story is good!

The end of the story, our story, is (and I'll say it again), "God wins!"

And if you choose to follow Jesus Christ and stay on God's side that means *you will win* too!

~*~

Reflection Questions:
1. How does it feel to know that God wins?
2. What will you do to stay on the winning side?

Week 44

Trusting God

"Some trust in chariots and some in horses, but we trust in the name of the Lord our God."

– Psalm 20:7 (NIV)

The song "Trust in You" by Anthony Brown & Group Therapy opens with lyrics to encourage the listener, declaring that God did not create us to worry or fear; He created us to worship Him and trust Him.

The song lyrics remind the listener about the magnitude of God. He is the King of Kings, Lord of Lords, Jehovah-jireh (our provider)! The music artists who perform this beautiful song emphasize God's glory to remind the believer just how big the God we serve is and that no problem that we face here on Earth is too big for God to solve! He's not just the Creator of the Universe; He is your Heavenly Father and He knows what is best for you.

The Bible says in Luke 12:7 that God numbered all of the hairs on our heads (and if you have a lot of hair on your head like I do then you know the significance of that saying). I think that this Bible verse means that God knows you more intimately than any human ever will and He is perfectly capable of meeting *all* of your needs!

God met my needs recently in a powerful way.

Late in January 2020, I asked all of the prayer warriors in my life to pray for me. I shared that I had been struggling to pay my bills after losing my job. I asked for prayer that God would bless me with more work that pays well so that I could pay my bills on time.

Less than five minutes later, prayer support and notes of encouragement started flooding in. Several people even shared their own stories about their struggles and how God came through for them just in the right time.

Among those prayer warriors were ones who said that they felt God leading them to give me a monetary gift and when I received their gift, it was just what I needed at that time.

This experience taught me several life lessons:

Lesson #1: Always go to God first. He loves you with ALL of His Heart and He cares about *everything* that impacts you here on Earth.

Lesson #2: Always feed your faith, not your fear. I made a point that morning after private prayer time with God to publicly post that song "Trust in You" and note that it's the new anthem to my *real* life story! I chose to praise God and trust Him to take care of me. I refused to give into to fear of the future based on my circumstances.

Lesson #3: Don't be afraid to ask for prayer support from the people in your life who believe in God and follow Jesus Christ. I did not ask for financial help but God impressed some people to send monetary gifts to me anyway. What a blessing!

Lesson #4: When God blesses you, don't stay silent! A few days after this amazing blessing and prayer support, God impressed me to write about my experience. I believe that He wants us to share our stories to encourage others who are going through similar situations. Our stories inspire hope!

On that note, I'd like for you to please know that no matter what you're facing in this life here on Earth, you *always* have hope because you have God. He loves you with all of His Heart, even if you don't know Him yet! That's why He sent His Son (Jesus Christ) to save you! Read John 3:16.

Following Jesus Christ and praying "the prayer of faith" (James 5:13-16) is something God wants all of us to do! Why? Because the Bible says in Hebrews 11:6 (NLT), "And it is impossible to please God without faith. Anyone who wants to come to him must believe that God exists and that he rewards those who sincerely seek him."

My "Word" for the New Year 2020 was "Trust." What a way to start the first month of that year with this teachable moment from God! After my experience in January 2020, I am encouraged to trust Him more and never stop praying about my every need because He cares and even when He's silent, He's there.

I hope that my testimony has encouraged your heart and inspired you to trust God with every need, every desire, every dream, and every plan for your life. Remember this: God is Good. God loves you and He will *never* leave you nor forsake you (Hebrews 13:5)!

May God bless your life story for His glory!

~*~

Reflection Questions:
1. When was the last time that God provided for your needs?
2. How does knowing that God answers your prayers, help you to trust Him?

Week 45

God's Waiting Room

"Wait for the Lord; be strong and take heart and wait for the Lord."

– Psalm 27:14 (NIV)

Since I was nine years old, I knew that I wanted to be a writer and producer when I grew up. At first, this dream of my heart meant that I wanted to write books that turned into movies. When I reached college, I found studying Print Journalism to be my sweet spot. After graduating from college and a summer internship at a faith-based magazine, God began taking me on several detours toward my dream career.

After graduating with my degree in Print Journalism, the journey to my creative career dreams has been filled with highs and lows. After being laid-off from my first day job where I worked as a schoolteacher, I transitioned into a job as full-time reporter for a county newspaper only a few months later and I loved it! However, after only five years on that job, the company went through severe budget cuts and had to let go of most of their freelance reporters, including me.

In the year before being laid-off from the newspaper, I decided to earn a degree that would get me closer to my dream career. I started grad school with Full Sail University during the summer of 2015 and within one year, I earned my MFA in Creative Writing. The week after graduation was when the newspaper laid me off from work. So I turned in my media pass and thought that maybe it was time for me to be my own boss. Therefore, I started my own business (Writer at Heart Editorial Services). The clients who I've worked with are happy with my work but I didn't have enough clients to make a solid living financially, which is why I continued to apply for another day job. However, the rejection letters keep rolling in.

I realized that God had me in what I like to call "God's Waiting Room." No, it's not a physical waiting room located in a hospital. It is more of a spiritual one where I'm waiting on my dreams to come true.

One day, I was sinking into despair but then in the midst of my worrying, God encouraged my heart when He led me to this song by Lincoln Brewster called "While I Wait." The song is essentially about waiting on the Lord and trusting Him with the outcome. It's also about trusting God in the process as you wait on Him to take you to where He wants you to be in life. This song taught me a few very important life lessons. Allow me to explain the lessons I'm learning while seated in God's Waiting Room.

If you're a human on planet Earth, you will have seasons of waiting. It varies from person to person. Some are waiting to graduate from school and enter the workforce. Some are waiting to marry their soul mate. Some newlyweds are waiting to purchase or build their dream home. Some married couples are waiting on a baby of their own. Some professionals are waiting on the job of their dreams. Some are waiting on peace to prevail in their land. Some are waiting on God to answer their prayers. We're all waiting on something or someone. While you're waiting, I want to encourage you to listen to this song by Lincoln Brewster called "While I Wait."

Here's what I've learned from the song and from my own experience of being in God's Waiting Room: Though I don't have the answers, I will trust God all the same. In his song "While I Wait," Lincoln Brewster says that sometimes miracles take time. I'm determined to worship God while I wait and will continue trusting Him. He makes miracles every day. It's only a matter of time before He makes one for me. I know this because God is faithful *every day*. His promises are permanent and He is faithful to fulfill each one. I don't understand the wait but I know that God is with me. I do not have all the answers but I serve a God who is sovereign, faithful and in control of my life story. He has the answers that I need. I'm trusting Him to reveal His will for my life in His perfect time.

So here's to everyone who's waiting on a dream of his or her heart to come true: Be encouraged. God loves you. He is Faithful to keep all of His promises that are found in His Word (The Holy Bible). If He made a promise to you then you can trust Him to keep it. It's like my Grandma used to say when she was alive, "God may not come when you want Him to but He's *always* on time!"

~*~

Reflection Questions:
1. How has trusting God helped you while you're waiting on Him?
2. What songs or Bible verses have helped to encourage you while you wait?

Week 46

The Wait is Over

> "But those who wait on the Lord
> Shall renew their strength;
> They shall mount up with wings like eagles,
> They shall run and not be weary,
> They shall walk and not faint."
>
> – Isaiah 40:31 (NKJV)

One of my Mom's favorite Bible verses is Isaiah 40:31. She recites it for family worship time every Sabbath. But it wasn't until recently that this verse became *very* real for me!

I've been through a season of waiting for my creative career dreams to come true ever since graduating from college. Since then, God has taken me on a journey of detours.

During those detours, I often asked God "Why do I have to do this?" and "When will my dreams come true?"

Looking back, I see how much God enriched my life through those detours. He gave me the opportunity to work with children from grades Pre-K through 12th grade. He built my business skills through seasonal employment in retail working for companies like Pottery Barn Kids, Williams-Sonoma and Macy's. He gave me the time to rest and make new friends in various career fields. One of my new friends who I met online through a Christian fellowship for women, told me during my waiting season that I have "the gift of time and friendship."

I realize now just how many beautiful blessings God gave to me that were not work-related but more for my personal growth. Blessings that made me feel loved and purposeful, showing me that my life had more meaning to it than just going to work, making a paycheck and climbing the career ladder.

Despite my not understanding what God was doing with my life as I waited on Him to make my creative career dreams come true, I chose to *trust Him*. I chose to continue believing that He has good plans for my life (Jeremiah 29:11).

After years of not knowing if I would ever get a job that pays well and allows me to use my skill set that I trained for in college, *the wait is over*! God provided me with a full-time job in Journalism in Summer 2019.

I will admit that during that waiting period, I certainly had my moments of emotional meltdowns, staying in bed for most of the day and feeling like my life was falling apart… but I chose to keep praying to God every day and night. I chose to encourage myself through Bible study and listening to Contemporary Christian and Gospel music. I chose to keep asking the prayer warriors in my life (my family, friends and pastors) to pray for me. And ultimately, I chose to *never give up*.

I do realize that this could have turned out another way. God could have chosen to *not* grant me the desires of my heart. He could have chosen to *not* give me a dream job in Journalism, which is what I earned my degree in, and I was prepared for that (often, I told God that anything He wants me to do, I will do it because He knows me better than I know myself).

However, God is a good God (Psalm 34:8) and He likes to give *good gifts* to His children (Matthew 7:11)! Yes, He may take you on detours. No, your original dreams many not come true. *But* you can *trust* that whatever He has planned for you (Jeremiah 29:11) is good, amazing and will help you feel like your life has purpose!

So as I close this devotional, I want to encourage you to continue trusting God. Continue seeking Him. Listen to this song by John Waller called "While I'm Waiting" and be encouraged that trusting God while you wait is the best idea!

The song lyrics basically say that we should worship God while we wait on Him to answer our prayers. It's not easy to wait on God but it's worth it. So please persevere, wait and trust God to answer your prayers. It can be painful to wait for certain things but God knows best and He wants you to move forward and continue to obey Him while you wait.

While you're in one of God's waiting rooms, ask Him how to, as my friend Quantrilla Ard told me, "honor Him in the wait." If He gives you the "gift of time and friendship" (as my friend Holly told me), then deeply inhale those precious blessings!

If God chooses to take you through trails and tribulations while you wait, keep pressing into Him and trusting that He'll never leave you nor forsake you (Hebrews 13:5)…and when He blesses you with your wildest dreams *or more than you could imagine*, always remember Him as you live out your God-given destiny!

~*~

Reflection Questions:
1. What are you waiting on God for in this life?
2. How does knowing that God always provides for us in His perfect time, encourage your heart while you wait?

Week 47

Melody at Midnight

"By day the Lord directs his love, at night his song is with me—a prayer to the God of my life."
– Psalm 42:8 (NIV)

God speaks to me through Contemporary Christian and Black Gospel music.

I always know He's sent me a message through song because often it's a song that I've heard before but all of a sudden, certain lyrics stand out to me.

These are always the lyrics that speak directly to my current situation, lyrics that didn't mean the same profound truth or provide the much-needed deep comfort as they did when I first listened to the song years in the past.

Sometimes, God sends devotional ideas by highlighting lyrics to the songs. Such is the case with today's devotional. The title I gave it is borrowed from a lyric from Kirk Franklin's song, "Why We Sing."

Somehow, though I've heard this song countless of times before, this part really stood out to me in November 2019. It's the line where Franklin declares: "You're my melody at midnight, Jesus!"

Instantly, my mind began to expound on that line in ways it never had before, and I knew that God wanted me to write this devotional.

Here's what I realized from that one line: No matter how dark trials in life may be, Jesus Christ is by your side and gives your heart a sweet song to sing! Why? Because you have *hope* when you have *Him* in your life! Following Jesus Christ will propel you into the promise of eternal life after human history ends and He returns to take His faithful followers home to Heaven.

Early in November 2019, one of my author friends (Angela Ruth Strong) shared that she was recently diagnosed with cancer. It's a disease that runs in her family so she knew it might be a challenge that she'd face one day but in no stretch of the imagination did she think that it would happen so soon! She's not near old age yet. But the doctors confirmed that she has breast cancer.

Angela is married to the man of her dreams named Jim and has three young adult children from her marriage to her first husband. She wants to see her children graduate from college, and she wants to be present for each child when they get married. It was definitely a dark time for Angela but she's surrounded by the love and support of her family and friends. But most importantly, she's being held by her Maker (God) who promises to carry Angela (and all of His children here on Earth) through uncertain times.

As I close this devotional, I'd like to encourage you to listen to the song "Why We Sing" and I'd like to invite you to pray for Angela.

Let's look at the message in the song lyrics written by Kirk Franklin: He speaks to people who may wonder why sometimes, churchgoers become emotional when singing praises to God and sometimes not everyone understands their praise. Then he breaks it down. He explains that they sing because they are happy and free in Jesus Christ. They sing because they realize that God loves them. They sing because the know that God's watches out for the sparrows and we are more important to Him than the birds of the air so we can rest assured that He watches out for us too! Nothing is wrong but we're crying as we're praising our Eternal King because God is good and His goodness to us despite our shortcomings is a beautiful truth that overwhelms us. And though the song may end with an hearty "Amen," we will not stop singing our songs to Jesus because we adore Him and appreciate all that He does for us. We want to praise Him for the rest of our life! After all, He gave us the breath of life and only He can save our soul!

In closing, I'd like to encourage you to remember that Jesus Christ wants to be your "melody at midnight." No matter how dark and challenging the trials of life are, you *always* have hope when God is in the picture ... and the *good news* is that God is *always in the picture*!

Be encouraged, sweet friends. The Creator of the Universe loves you!

~*~

Reflection Questions:
1. Remember a time when God was there for you in pain and sorrow. How did knowing that He was on your side make you feel?
2. What is your favorite song to sing to Jesus? Why?

Week 48

Perfect Christians

> "But without faith it is impossible to please him: for he that cometh to God must believe that he is, and that he is a rewarder of them that diligently seek him."
>
> – Hebrews 11:6 (KJV)

It was a perfect fall day with crisp air in the atmosphere, beautiful scenery (love the changing colors of the leaves) and weather warm but cool enough to wear my favorite tan color boots. I had a great day but I was hit by anxiety as I reflected on how lately, I as the quintessential perfectionist, felt like I was falling short of being perfect and therefore disappointing God.

As I drove down the road in my car alone, I felt God impress me with these words, "It's not about you being perfect. It's about you having faith in Me." Those words rocked my reality in a good and needed way because I realized that I'll never be the "perfect" Christian completely because I'm only human and we live in a broken world.

Nobody is perfect—not me, not you, not the most capable people in the world—but there is a God, a Lord and Savior who is perfect and sinless—His name is Jesus Christ. I'm learning to look to Him as my refuge and thank Him for His grace and mercy that kept me because even on my best days when I think I've done my best and am close to perfection, I still will never be good enough—or sinless enough—to make it to Heaven without an active, steadfast faith in God.

According to Isaiah 64:6 (KJV), all of our righteousness is like "filthy rags." It's our faith and obedience to God that helps us make it to Heaven, not our best efforts of trying to be perfect while here on planet Earth. We live in a broken world. People are suffering and nobody's perfect, not even the most "perfect" Christians, which is why it's important to follow Christ, not Christians.

When he was living, the famous Mahatma Gandhi said, "I like your Christ, I do not like your Christians. Your Christians are so unlike your Christ."

It is understandable that Gandhi felt disappointed by what he saw in Christians because nobody is perfect. But it is also dangerous for anyone to go through life avoiding Christ because they do not like Christians, since we are called to follow Jesus Christ, not Christians. Anytime you put your full faith and trust in humankind, you're bound to be disappointed because only Jesus can truly save you and only God has the innate and long-lasting capability to never let you down.

God is not looking for Perfect Christians. He is looking for faithful followers, people who take up their cross and die to their fleshly desires daily (Matthew 16:24).

In closing, I'd like to share a song by my Mom's favorite gospel artist, CeCe Winans. One of the songs that CeCe sings has special meaning for my Mom and for this devotional. The song is called "His Strength is Perfect."

The song essentially says that God's strength is perfect because He helps us to carry on through the trials of life and when we're too weak to walk on our own, He carries us. The Bible says that when we are weak, God is strong. Let's read about it in 2 Corinthians 12:9-10 (KJV): "And he said unto me, My grace is sufficient for thee: for my strength is made perfect in weakness. Most gladly therefore will I rather glory in my infirmities, that the power of Christ may rest upon me. Therefore I take pleasure in infirmities, in reproaches, in necessities, in persecutions, in distresses for Christ's sake: for when I am weak, then am I strong."

We can rely on God's mercy and grace to carry us when we are weary. The song "His Strength is Perfect," reminds us that this life is about God, not us. It's not about our success stories or personal glories. Our life here on Earth is about realizing that when we are weak, we can lean on God because His strength is perfect and He'll help us through the trials of life. When we are at our end and we rely on Him. *He* is our refuge and strength (Psalm 46:1).

Isn't that beautiful? Let's celebrate this truth and remember that God isn't calling us to be perfect, He's calling us to be faithful.

~*~

Reflection Questions:
1. How does knowing and trusting Jesus Christ help you when you feel the pressure to be perfect?
2. How has God carried you through tough times in your life?

Week 49

Not My Home

"For this world is not our permanent home; we are looking forward to a home yet to come."

– Hebrews 13:14 (NLT)

On the drive home years ago, my mind was inundated with the injustices, tragedy and pain in this world that we as humans experience.

As my mind delved deeper into despair, I spoke these words aloud: "Earth is *not* my home. If I can just remember that, I'll be fine."

And just like that, I realized that God had given me a message for this devotional with the key phrase, "Not My Home."

People who believe in God and follow His Son Jesus Christ know that this planet Earth is *not* our home. We look forward to our *true* home in Heaven. It's a perfect place free of sin and all of its side effects: death, disease, injustice, oppression, pain, etc.

There's a Bible story in the book of Hebrews that resonates with me as I write this devotional. The story is about a man named Abraham who was called to go to a place where he would later receive as his inheritance (Hebrews 11:8, NIV).

God told him to go to a foreign land and by faith Abraham went without hesitation and made his home in the Promised Land. Now the verse that speaks to my writer heart most profoundly is Hebrews 11:10 (NIV), which says, "For he was looking forward to the city with foundations, whose architect and builder is God."

As Christians that's our eternal hope: We are looking forward to our Promised Land, "the city with foundations, whose architect and builder is God." How beautiful is that? God is the Architect and Builder of our Heavenly Home. His home is peaceful and perfect because He designed it and His establishments are sin-free.

I look forward to the day when God puts a permanent end to sin. I look forward to Jesus Christ returning to take His faithful followers home. Honestly, most days it's the only hope that gets me through. This world is getting worse, as the Bible tells us it will before Christ returns. But we have hope!

According to Wayne Hooper who wrote "We Have This Hope" (a church hymn), "We have this hope that burns within our hearts, hope in the coming of the Lord!"

We can rest assure that if we accept Jesus Christ's gift of salvation and follow Him while we're living on this Earth, then we will go home to Heaven with Him when He returns. We can trust that He will destroy the devil, the evil angels and all who follow the devil. We can know that after that final act happens, evil will no longer exist—peace and pure bliss like you've never known it before will reign forever.

The Bible says in Revelation 21:4 (NKJV), "God will wipe away every tear from their eyes; there shall be no more death, nor sorrow, nor crying. There shall be no more pain, for the former things have passed away."

Now that is a hope to hold on to, a promise of a better time, a better place that is not of this world! Honestly, this reminds me of the song "Another Time, Another Place" by Sandi Patty and Wayne Watson. They sing about how they've heard stories about a distant land that is far beyond human imagination. It's a place free of pain, sorrow, heartache and tears of sadness. They say that this beautiful place is lit by an everlasting light that is pure and holy ... a place free from fear, trial and tribulations ... a place where their heart and soul yearns to be. It is a place that they as Christ followers only get a glimpse of while journeying on this planet Earth. Ultimately, this place is Heaven which is the true home of all those who believe in God and follow Jesus Christ. But for now, until that time comes when Jesus takes us to Heaven, we must make it through our journey here on Earth.

The good news is that there is hope for humankind as we journey through this dark world because God is Good. He keeps His promises and just like He promised, He *will* return to take us home to that perfect place. Until then, stay in tune with Him and let Him lead you.

There are so many hurting people in this world. Ask God how He can use you to help others. He wants us to occupy until He returns (Luke 19:13 KJV). Let His Light in you shine brightly in this dark world. Let His Light lead others to His heart and inspire Hope in their hurting hearts.

Earth is not our home. Heaven is our final destination. Let's live like it.

~*~

Reflection Questions:
1. Have you ever felt overwhelmed by the woes of this world?
2. In what ways can you focus on Heaven and eternal hope when you feel overwhelmed?

Week 50

Preparing for Heaven

"For God so loved the world that he gave his one and only Son, that whoever believes in him shall not perish but have eternal life."

– John 3:16 (NIV)

American author Hamilton Wright Mabie is famous for this saying that truly encapsulates the Christmas season. He said, "Blessed is the season which engages the whole world in a conspiracy of love."

While preparing the house for Christmas one year, my Mom and I scurried about, setting up the traditional Christmas tree (ours is not real), filling the house with festive decorations, bright lights and Christmas items throughout all while playing her Christmas music that was popular in the 70's and still resonates today, a thought occurred to me: *Are we preparing for Heaven?*

Just like people around the world prepare for this Christmas season weeks and sometimes months in advance and they take it seriously, are we as Christ-followers serious about preparing for The Second Coming of Jesus Christ?

It is an event that we all must take seriously because there is no other option than heaven or hell. You're either accepting Christ's gift of salvation then choosing to follow Him which means you're going to Heaven or you're allowing the temporary trappings of this world to indulge you and you're being led astray by the enemy of Christ whose only intention is to lead you to hell. The enemy knows how beautiful Heaven is. He also knows how much God loves you and wants you to be there. The enemy is aware that when his time is up, he's bound to hell and he wants to take you there with him. Don't be fooled by the guises of the devil.

Remember that there is a loving God who created you and wants you to be reconciled to Him. Reject the ways of the world that are against God and embrace His plan for your life. God's plan for you includes restoration and eternal life. You can trust that it's filled with more than this world in its sin-affected state can offer. The Bible says that no eye has seen nor ear has heard nor has the mind imagined what God has prepared for those who love Him (1 Corinthians 2:9)! God's way may look strict when you compare it with the ways of this world, but if you remember that He wants to protect you and save your soul—and that in the end, He *wins*—then the future is brighter than Christmas lights. You will be okay and stay within the boundaries that He set to keep you safe *and* saved!

Years ago, I saw cartoon about a man who was racing toward the end of a cliff, only he didn't *know* it was a *cliff*. If he kept going full speed ahead, he would fall to his death. His friend, who saw the life-threatening danger ahead, was chasing after him shouting at him to stop, warning him that he was going to die if he kept on going. The illustration was to show that this is us! It's our human condition. We race for the things in life we think that we want. We are mesmerized by the glamorization of sin. We think that our own way is the best, but the Bible says in Proverbs 14:12 (KJV), "There is a way which seemeth right unto a man, but the end thereof are the ways of death." But often, all we can see with our finite minds is the glamour and the allure of sin so we keep pursuing it because we want more but what we don't realize is that at the end of that pursuit of worldly happiness is death.

The Bible says in John 3:16 (NIV), "For God so loved the world that he gave his one and only Son, that whoever believes in him shall not perish but have eternal life."

There is a beautiful Christmas song based on that Bible verse. The song is called "For God So Loved." Jasmine Murray performs my favorite version of this song. She opens the song with mention of the festivities and decorations of Christmastime. She speaks of the beautiful glow of Christmas lights and the magical feeling this holiday season brings. She mentions the expectation that's in the air not just for kids, but for adults! But then she speaks of a truth greater than Christmas; she tells the listener about God and how He so loved the world that He sent His Son (Jesus Christ) to show us the way to eternal life. At the end of her song, she reminds the listener that the greatest gift of all is Jesus Christ.

Falling in love with Jesus is better than falling in love with this Christmas season. Because unlike the holidays, a life with Christ in the center of it is something you can take from earth to Heaven. His love for you spans eternity. Won't you choose Him this Christmas? Salvation given by Jesus Christ is the *best* gift you'll ever receive because it will result in eternal life!

Yes, *blessed* is this beautiful holiday season but *greater* is God's unconditional, eternal love for you. Unwrap the best gift this Christmas (a relationship with Jesus Christ) and allow Him to lead you through this life.

~*~

Reflection Questions:
1. Will you accept the best gift you could ever receive this Christmas (a relationship with Jesus Christ)?
2. Are you preparing for Heaven?

Week 51

God's Gift: Paid in Full

> "For the wages of sin is death; but the gift of God is eternal life through Jesus Christ our Lord."
>
> – Romans 6:23 (KJV)

"Jesus Paid It All" by Passion featuring Kristian Stanfill is a beautiful song that resonates with me.

The Christmas holiday season reminds me not just about the *birth* of Jesus Christ but of His sacrifice that saved our souls! Read about it in John 3:16-17 then read the entire Bible for the complete context.

For the purposes of this devotional, I am going to focus on one key concept based on the title and lyrics to the song "Jesus Paid It All." As the song says (and I paraphrase): Jesus paid it all! Yes, the wages of sin *is* death but Jesus Christ (God's Son) made a way for us to be saved and receive eternal life! We only have to accept God's gift of salvation through His Son Jesus, believe in God and follow Jesus all the way to Heaven.

December 2019 was a bit challenging for me because I was in between jobs and I didn't know how I was going to pay my overdue cell phone bill. Other bills took priority, including two unexpected expenses.

I called my phone service and asked if they could extend the overdue payment deadline. They said that the latest they could extend it to was December 20. But two days before it was due, I still didn't have the money that I needed to pay my phone bill. So I decided to pray to God about it and let it go, knowing that God would provide.

Later on that day, while I was in the kitchen washing the dishes, I heard my cell phone make the sound that let me know I had received a text message. I walked over to the kitchen table and picked up my phone. The message read that my overdue cell phone bill was paid in full!

The receipt showed the last four digits of the card number that was used to pay my bill. I was happy but confused at the same time because the card number was not one of my own and I couldn't think of anyone who had the information necessary to pay my bill for me. After all, I'd only told my dad a day before that it looked like my cell phone would be out of service until I figured out how to pay the overdue amount.

Five minutes later, my dad returned home, presented a receipt to me and said "Merry Christmas!"

I accepted the receipt and received my answer: The receipt showed the same last four digits of the card number that was in the text message on my phone. The overdue amount was highlighted and noted that it was paid in full. My dad had paid my debt! He said that God led him to do that for me.

As the song "Jesus Paid It All" filled my mind, I realized a spiritual parallel to this blessing: As a free gift, God paid the debt for my sins when He sent His Son Jesus Christ to this Earth to show humankind the way to our Heavenly

Father (John 14:6). God allowed Jesus to live, die then be resurrected to serve as our High Priest in Heaven.

If it were *not* for Christ's sacrifice and God's Love for us, we'd be doomed. We'd never make it to Heaven. We'd never be reunited with our Creator and we'd never experience the joys of what's to come (eternal life forever in the presence of our Savior as we enjoy a truly perfect, sin-free, pain-free, death-free existence). The Bible says in 1 Corinthians 2:9 (ESV): But, as it is written, "What no eye has seen, nor ear heard, nor the heart of man imagined, what God has prepared for those who love him."

God has great things planned for all who believe in Him and accept His Son Jesus Christ as The Way, The Truth and The Life (John 14:6)!

Just like my Heavenly Father (God) inspired my earthly father (my Dad) to pay my cell phone bill in full so that weight would be lifted off of me and I could be free from having to pay that debt that I could not afford, God sent His Son Jesus Christ to save our life by paying a debt that none of us (no matter how wealthy or determined or perfect) could pay (because we're all sinners in need of a Savior). All you and I have to do is to accept God's gift to us that He paid in full.

Isn't it beautiful when you receive a gift that has been *paid in full*?

~*~

Reflection Questions:
1. How does it feel to know that Jesus paid your debt in full?
2. In what ways can you pay it forward and tell the world about the free gift of salvation offered through Jesus Christ's sacrifice?

Week 52

The Gathering

Jesus answered, "Everyone who drinks this water will be thirsty again, but whoever drinks the water I give them will never thirst. Indeed, the water I give them will become in them a spring of water welling up to eternal life."

– John 4:13-14 (NIV)

Shopping a few days after Christmas with my Mom at our favorite mall, I noticed a big crowd congregating inside a store, poring over the latest technology. I looked up and saw that the store was nameless. There was no visible sign to describe what it was, so I turned to my Mom and asked, "Is that an Apple Store?" My mom immediately said, "Of course. What other store brings people together like that?"

A light bulb turned on and I made an instant connection between that reality and our reality as mere mortals living in a fallen world. It is very common for people to crowd into an Apple Store and pore over all the latest technology. However, it is very *uncommon* for people to flock to church, fill the pews from the front to the back of the sanctuary, and press into Jesus Christ, allowing His restoring love to pour into our broken hearts.

Why is it that we're so quick to get the latest technology and stay up to date with it at an Apple Store, but so reluctant to read a Bible and stay in touch with the Author (God)?

I know that we all may be guilty of not spending enough time with God. But think about it. We make time for what matters to us and God should matter most.

People gather religiously at sporting events, favorite stores, cafes, restaurants, and movie theaters. Why don't people flock to church to gather together before the Lord?

Jesus brings people together. His Gathering is of greater purpose than The Apple Store. Why pore over new technology like your life depends on it when you can pore over God's Word and be transformed from the inside out? Most importantly, our life *does* depend on it.

When Jesus Christ ministered here on Earth, large crowds gathered to hear Him preach about the now and the not yet. He told stories that taught kingdom principles—God's Kingdom principles.

Jesus served food that never faded. He served heavenly manna (Matthew 4:4), words of wisdom to help get you through this life on Earth. His words can help you get into Heaven.

Best of all, Jesus is not just a Bible character. He is real. Those characters whose stories are told in the Bible are dead now but the Lord still lives! And He is constantly wooing our hearts to His. He wants us to gather around Him, learn from His life lessons then go tell the world about Him and His saving grace.

So won't you gather before the Lord in His church? All He asks is for you to meet Him there once a week. But He does not want church to be your only interaction with Him. He wants you to daily spend time in His presence, read

His Word (The Holy Bible) that's better than all the latest technology, and follow His instructions.

Most of all, He wants you to tell the world about Him because His Gathering is all-inclusive. He wants *everyone* to be saved.

I found that going to God's Gathering refreshes my soul and renews my spirit. I can get from God want I cannot get from the Apple Store. I can get peace that passes all understanding (Philippians 4:7), complete joy (John 15:11), and guidance from this life to the next (Proverbs 3:5-6).

Best of all, Jesus invites you to "Come just as you are" which means you don't have to be perfect or perfectly put together in appearance to go to His gathering. He welcomes you as you are, with open arms! He will not judge you on your past mistakes and condemn you for being a sinner. He looks past the sin and loves the sinner.

However, He doesn't want you to stay in your sins because that leads to destruction. Jesus wants you to come to Him as you are and allow Him to change you for the better from the inside out! I can testify to that as someone who has personally gone through that transformation. I am forever grateful to God for renovating me from the inside out. He renewed my mind (Romans 12:2), filled my heart with His hope and blessed my mind with His peace that passes all understanding (Philippians 4:7). He gave me a genuine love for His people (those who do know him and those who do not know Him yet) and He made me feel secure in His love for me. Jesus wants to do that for you too!

There's a beautiful song that's like what we church goers call an "altar call" which is an opportunity for people who were touched by the pastor's sermon to "come to Jesus." The song is called "Come Just As You Are." Let's focus on the version sung by Crystal Lewis. The lyrics invite the listener to come to Jesus just as they are (you don't have to be sinless or look perfect) and receive His Living Water then never thirst again!

Basically, this means that when you receive Jesus Christ into your life, not only will He give you strength to make it through each day, He'll give you hope! His presence in your life will satisfy your deepest thirst in way that not even the most pure drinking water or the most treasured relationship with a human here on Earth can. Only Jesus can quench the thirst of your soul.

Won't you go to God's Gathering? He's waiting to welcome you with open arms!

~*~

Reflection Questions:
1. How does it feel to know that God wants to spend quality time with you?
2. Will you go to God's Gathering?

Author Bio

Alexis A. Goring is a writer at heart and journalist by profession.

She loves the storytelling process, including everything from interviewing people for news media and faith-based publications to writing the story, editing the story and publishing the story.

Alexis is an author of Inspirational Romance fiction stories and nonfiction devotionals that inspire the heart. She has written and published three fiction books and her devotionals have appeared in numerous faith-based publications. *Stories and Songs of Faith: My Journey with God* is her first nonfiction book project filled with original devotionals that she wrote.

Always up for a new adventure, Alexis has traveled to Italy where she explored the culture, food and language with friends. She even moved to Montana where the air is fresh and the land is beautiful, to take her first big break in Journalism as the Editor and Reporter for a county newspaper.

Photography is another passion that's close to her heart. Alexis enjoys using her camera to capture the genuine emotions that people naturally display on joyous occasions. She is experienced in natural light photography and photojournalism.

Music is another passion that Alexis has loved forever. Listening to movie soundtracks from her favorite productions feels like a hug for her heart. She loves it when the bridge of a song makes you feel like you're taking flight!

A total foodie, Alexis not only enjoys eating delicious food at her favorite restaurants, but she's also a talented baker and chef.

At the end of the day, Alexis hopes that her love for Jesus Christ will shine through all of her creative endeavors. She prays that her writing will warm hearts and point people to God who loves them with all of His Heart!

You can learn more about Alexis as a creative professional by visiting her official website https://alexisagoring.jimdo.com.

Song Directory

Week 1
God's Family: A Forever Place to Belong
Songs:
"Your Love Never Fails" by Chris Quilala / Jesus Culture - Jesus Culture Music
Link: https://youtu.be/IoezWBPGRAc

"God's Family" by Tommy Walker
Link: https://youtu.be/ax47qefwRRY

Week 2
Always Welcome
Song: "Throne Room" by CeCe Winans
Link: https://youtu.be/jafqmQP79PQ

Week 3
God As our Guide
Song: "You're Gonna Be Okay" by Brian & Jenn Johnson
Link: https://youtu.be/LjF9IqvXDjY

Week 4
A God Who Hears
Song: "Every Single Tear" by Scott Krippayne
Link: https://youtu.be/mxIjpkTcNvY

Week 5
Jesus is Here
Songs:
"O Come to the Altar" by Elevation Worship
Link: https://youtu.be/rYQ5yXCc_CA

"Here Today" by Scott Krippayne
Link: https://youtu.be/zy-7iVclhSc

Week 6
BE The Message
Song: "People Need the Lord" by Steve Green
Link: https://youtu.be/t8bu2dnwypQ

Week 7
Our Greatest Resource
Song: "Healing" by Richard Smallwood
Link: https://youtu.be/fEadw8gm9RY

Week 8
Making Room for God
Song: "Make Room" by Jonathan McReynolds
Link: https://youtu.be/U05dCZueoeM

Week 9
Silver Platter Faith
Song: "The Anchor Holds" by Ray Boltz
Link: https://youtu.be/MSAc5Z2lprk

Week 10
Knowing Jesus
Song: "All I Once Held Dear" by Robin Mark
Link: https://youtu.be/oxpPIa-BskY

Week 11
Kings and Kingdoms
Songs:
"There's Something About That Name" (Live) by Bill & Gloria Gaither
Link: https://youtu.be/cwzP1jiYhi0

"I Surrender All" by Clay Crosse
Link: https://youtu.be/THHu5QPjB_4

Week 12
Hope for a Broken World

Song: "Is He Worthy?" by Andrew Peterson
Link: https://youtu.be/OIahc83Kvp4

Week 13
Out of Darkness and Into the Light
Song: "God With Us" by Terrian
Link: https://youtu.be/PJbtWOSYjBM

Week 14
The Greatest Countdown
Song: "We Have This Hope" by Wayne Hooper
Link: https://youtu.be/gkjBLFGBGSM

Week 15
Spartans and Soldiers for Christ: Be A Finisher
Motivational Track: "I Can Handle It" by Pastor Steven Furtick of Elevation Church
Link: https://youtu.be/P8kgbpR1fSc

Week 16
A Masterpiece in the Making
Song: "He Who Began A Good Work in You" by Steve Green
Link: https://youtu.be/eNjZlHARnEk

Week 17
Strength for the Journey
Song: "There is A Name" by Byron Cage
Link: https://youtu.be/l8ANIlyW34g

Week 18
God's Hand
Song: "He Has His Hands On You" by Marvin Sapp
Link: https://youtu.be/AzT6MQRi2Js

Week 19
Made in His Image

Song: "Measure of A Man" by 4Him
Link: https://youtu.be/OJAsNIh1gEU

Week 20
Respect and the God who deserves it
Song: "What A Beautiful Name" by Brooklyn Tabernacle Choir
Link: https://youtu.be/6Yc3exCsHCw

Week 21
Friends in High Places: My Reflections inspired by the song
Song: "Friends in High Places" by Larnelle Harris
Link: https://youtu.be/nsUFT6d8q2w

Week 22
Words of Life
Song: "Ancient Words" by Michael W. Smith
Link: https://youtu.be/3vmTkXNpwzs

Week 23
Influencers for Christ
Song: "I Will Follow Christ" by Clay Crosse, Bebe Winans & Bob Carlisle
Link: https://youtu.be/BdD4uoHKW38

Week 24
Acknowledgements from God in the Lamb's Book of Life
Song: "I Am Not Ashamed" by Heritage Singers
Link: https://youtu.be/ShRG0lDAiCE

Week 25
God Knows Your Name
Song: "He Knows My Name" by Francesca Battistelli
Link: https://youtu.be/jYpBgJHmGmw

Week 26
Wearing God's Name

Song: "Wear Your Name" by Gylchris Sprauve
Link: https://youtu.be/AWtzEAhFb4c

Week 27
Sabbath Rest
Song: "Sabbath Day" by The AsidorS
Link: https://youtu.be/84ZCvnHnBxk

Week 28
God's Protection
Song: "Angels Watching Over Me" by Virtue
Link: https://youtu.be/c9zu_XTpxnM

Week 29
The Christian Life
Motivational Track: "I Will Fight" by Pastor Steven Furtick of Elevation Church
Motivational Track Link:
https://www.youtube.com/watch?v=XyzG7F-CS7U

Week 30
What's Your Motivation?
Song: "Lord I'm Ready Now" by Plumb
Link: https://youtu.be/zBUQqLp6N24

Week 31
A Happily Ever After that Never Ends
Song: "Forever" by Kari Jobe
Link: https://youtu.be/huFra1mnIVE

Week 32
Enduring Love
Song: "God Loves You" by Jaci Velasquez
Link: https://youtu.be/kzUqlTKdqlk

Week 33
A Different Kind of Overwhelmed

Song: "Into Words" by Jasmine Murray
Link: https://youtu.be/2VbSIp1n-4M

Week 34
Our Forever Friend
Song: "Forever Yours" by Wintley Phipps
Link: https://youtu.be/Ra83WQGxvsQ

Week 35
God's Not Going Anywhere
Song: "He's Always There" by CeCe Winans
Link: https://youtu.be/yn16S0_LYpU

Week 36
God's Nudge
Song: "He Knows My Name" by Maranatha Singers
Link: https://youtu.be/hXsiWoyjw60

Week 37
Before I Call
Song: "When God's People Pray" by Wayne Watson
Link: https://youtu.be/KuEWnSto1YY

Week 38
On the Clock God
Song: "My Help (Cometh from the Lord)" by Brooklyn Tabernacle Choir
Link: https://youtu.be/k47xB8eoT5g

Week 39
Shelter in the Rain
Song: "A Shelter in the Time of Storm" by Vernon J. Charlesworth
Link: https://youtu.be/dn-tofXF_Ko

Week 40
The Rich Life

STORIES AND SONGS OF FAITH

Song: "Can't Live A Day" by Avalon
Link: https://youtu.be/EjyMY5hdU84

Week 41
Eternal Awards
Song: "The Best is Yet to Come" by Scott Krippayne
Link: https://youtu.be/FyaL7Hsstc0

Week 42
Glimpses of Heaven
Song: "When It's All Been Said and Done" by Robin Mark
Link: https://youtu.be/1llIIhBMCjU

Week 43
End of Story
Song: "Heaven's Door" by Dwight Anderson
Link: https://youtu.be/gIp23IxwTm0

Week 44
Trusting God
Song: "Trust in You" by Anthony Brown & Group Therapy
Link: https://youtu.be/jzvNPeL5Kuc

Week 45
God's Waiting Room
Song: "While I Wait" by Lincoln Brewster
Link: https://youtu.be/NswPPVgMaPE

Week 46
The Wait is Over
Song: "While I'm Waiting" by John Waller
Link: https://youtu.be/q0F2pyZyjdo

Week 47
Melody at Midnight
Song: "Why We Sing" by Kirk Franklin
Link: https://youtu.be/kZosEgdE-mo

Week 48
Perfect Christians
Song: "His Strength is Perfect" by CeCe Winans
Link: https://youtu.be/Cht9lgBQJCQ

Week 49
Not My Home
Song: "Another Time, Another Place" by Sandi Patty and Wayne Watson
Link: https://youtu.be/A_0K98XSwCw

Week 50
Preparing for Heaven
Song: "For God So Loved" by Jasmine Murray
Link: https://youtu.be/Lp6DWSzzqz4

Week 51
God's Gift: Paid in Full
Song: "Jesus Paid It All" (Lyrics And Chords/Live) by Passion ft. Kristian Stanfill
Link: https://youtu.be/0rWXUqF_BFo

Week 52
The Gathering
Song: "Come Just As You Are" by Crystal Lewis
Link: https://youtu.be/V6DP5TPz81c

Made in the USA
Middletown, DE
25 April 2024